## Praise for Marketing Workbook for Nonprofit Organizations Volume II...

"Mobilizing people for marketing success is one of the greatest challenges facing social sector leaders. Only when we are prepared for action can social sector organizations produce their vital bottom line, changed lives. Gary Stern's workbook leads us through the essential marketing process and the *Pocket Guide* makes sure we don't leave home without his guidance. Effective marketing is not only for the corporate world; it's also an indispensable responsibility of the social sector organization. Gary Stern leads the way to making every member of our organization, volunteer and staff, paid and unpaid, an effective marketing representative."

— *Frances Hesselbein, President and CEO*
*Peter F. Drucker Foundation for Nonprofit Management*

"For the past year we have been working with Gary Stern and the 'Stern Method' and I can report that we are truly changing the way we think about our work. *Marketing Workbook Volume I* is in broad use in Lung Associations throughout the country. *Marketing Workbook Volume II* incorporates the same step-by-step approach to building winning relationships."

— *Joseph Bergen, Deputy Managing Director*
*American Lung Association*

"Attracting and retaining top volunteer leaders are two of the greatest challenges nonprofits face today. Gary Stern gets to the core of the matter with a sound program that combines the best of human psychology, strategic market wizardry, and basic common sense. In addition to being an excellent tool for developing and cultivating a volunteer workforce, the book reflects Gary's own warm witty style that has captivated every national audience of United Way volunteers and staff to which he has spoken. Volume II is an indispensable companion to the equally indispensable (and very dog-eared) *Marketing Workbook for Nonprofit Organizations Volume I.*"

— *Martina A. Martin, Vice President of Strategic Planning, Marketing and Government Affairs, United Way of Central Maryland*

"This manual positions marketing as a viable and necessary program in which all not-for-profits need to engage. It provides an economical, systematic, easy-to-read guide focusing on 'people power' rather than 'dollar power' for marketing the case."

— *Patricia F. Lewis, ACRFE, President and CEO*
*National Society of Fund Raising Executives*

"*Marketing Workbook for Nonprofit Organizations Volume II: Mobilize People for Marketing Success* is a comprehensive guide to help organizations create new resources through the cultivation of their people. In a detailed manner, the workbook walks both the novice and seasoned marketing practitioner through ways to unleash the promotional power inherent in employees, volunteers, board members, and friends of the organization. The strategic approach, practical worksheets and appendices, and wide array of social and nonprofit marketing examples make the guide highly recommended reading for anyone who wants to expand the marketing reach and impact of their nonprofit organization."

— *Sonya A. Grier, Assistant Professor of Marketing*
*Stanford University Graduate School of Business*

*Marketing Workbook for Nonprofit Organizations Volume II:*

# Mobilize People for Marketing Success

by Gary J. Stern

Author of *Marketing Workbook for Nonprofit
Organizations Volume I: Develop the Marketing Plan*

Published by Amherst H. Wilder Foundation
Saint Paul, Minnesota

The Amherst H. Wilder Foundation is one of the largest
and oldest endowed human services and community
development organizations in America. For more than
ninety years, the Wilder Foundation has been providing
health and human services that help children and families grow strong, the elderly age with dignity, and the
community grow in its ability to meet its own needs.

For information about other Wilder Foundation publications, please see the order form on the last page or
contact:

Publishing Center
Amherst H. Wilder Foundation
919 Lafond Avenue
Saint Paul, MN  55104
1-800-274-6024

Edited by Vincent Hyman
Illustrated by Rick Peterson
Designed by Rebecca Andrews

Manufactured in the United States of America

First printing, August 1997

Library of Congress Catalog Card Number: 90-83183

ISBN 0-940-06910-5

To Tom Olson, who always knows what it's about.

# Acknowledgments

With grateful acknowledgment to Vince Hyman who provided invaluable editing and in every way helped the author stay the course.

To Becky Andrews, who makes a book a palace.

With special thanks to Audrey Anderson, Kirsten Lukens, Paul Rengstorf, Jenny Morgenthau, Louise Wolfgram, Independent Sector, and my family.

And with gratitude to all those kind enough to review and comment on the manuscript:

Carol Aquino, Sam Asher, Alida Baker, Bryan Barry, Roger Beaubien, Joe Bergen, H. Yvonne Cheek, Karen Lee Davis, John Easley, Linda Ewing, Sharon Farsht, Jill Friedman Fixler, Iris Freeman, Toni Green, Susan Gunderson, Paul Irving, Beverly Klegman, Nancy Latimer, Anne Long, Carol Lukas, Karin McElwain, Sam Modenstein, Mike Newman, Jean Nierenhausen, Jackie Norris, Karen Ray, Timothy Rose, Nora Silver, Anne Smith, Christy Stolpestad, Jim Stone, Sarah Strickland, Terri Swanson, Roger Toogood, and Marjorie Weiser.

# About the Author

Gary J. Stern is president of Gary J. Stern & Associates, Inc., an international consulting firm specializing in marketing, strategic planning, and organization development with nonprofit groups. He is a frequent keynote speaker and trainer and the author of three books including *Marketing Workbook for Nonprofit Organizations Volume I,* which has sold 30,000 copies, is in circulation in more than thirty-five countries, and was adapted as the official marketing workbook of United Way of America.

Formerly senior consultant with the Amherst H. Wilder Foundation, Gary's clients include The American Lung Association, The Fresh Air Fund, National Council of Jewish Women, Children's Home Society of Minnesota, The United Way of Canada—Centraide Canada, and many more. He has been a guest lecturer at the Stanford University Graduate School of Business and was a featured presenter in the 1995 Peter F. Drucker Foundation Leadership Conference, "Serving Customers, Changing Lives."

# Contents

# Mobilize People for Success

Consider these findings from a 1994 Gallup Poll conducted for the nonprofit research and advocacy group Independent Sector:

- *People are more than twice as likely to give when asked than when they are not.*
- *People are more than four times as likely to volunteer when asked than when they are not.*

Sounds basic: nonprofits who want more support need to get out there and ask for it. But who does the asking? Traditionally, a precious few. Whether seeking members, enrollment, attendance, in-kind gifts, volunteers, funds, or other responses, most nonprofits make *asking* the province of a small corps of staff specialists and the rare volunteer. No matter how dedicated or skilled, a handful of people can never keep up.

Today's trends mandate change from this self-limiting approach. Some mistakenly complain of shrinking resources, but the former "pie" isn't the problem. Old growth support remains, it simply has limits. Nonprofits must continue tending to existing sources of support and simultaneously set their sights on the resource-rich potential in new relationships. It's first a matter of making sure *you have something of value to offer*—of aligning programs and services to meet today's wants, needs, and aspirations. Then it's a matter of igniting the grassroots power in your own backyard *to ask for what you need.*

> It's a matter of igniting the grassroots power in your own backyard *to ask for what you need.*

## "People buy from people"

Living in a super-charged, multimedia world, it's easy to think marketing victories go mainly to the Web-wise and televised. Granted, the Internet is promising, media are powerful, and the ability to reach millions per minute—when we can afford it—a decided plus. But none of this holds a candle to the most persuasive medium of all: *personal contact.* The sales-world adage, *people buy from people,* is more meaningful today than ever before. A postcard, phone call, face-to-face visit—even E-mail from *someone we know*—cuts through, gets our attention, and is more likely than anything to compel us to act. This point was recently driven home to me when a friend delivered an invitation to a sponsorship party for his upcoming five hundred mile AIDS bike ride. I couldn't make the party, but he got a check on the spot. It was *him,* face-to-face, that did it. He single-handedly went on to raise $5,000, and there are many more like him who, together, bring in millions.

Here are more headline results from pioneering nonprofits who expanded the ranks of people directly involved in promoting their cause:

> The most persuasive medium of all: *personal contact.*

ENROLLMENT JUMPS 10 PERCENT THROUGH
FACULTY-MOUNTED RECRUITMENT EFFORT

VOLUNTEER HOST FAMILIES EXPAND OWN RANKS TO
WELCOME NYC KIDS FOR SUMMER BREAK

TRUSTEES SPEARHEAD $50 MILLION
MUSEUM CAPITAL DRIVE

BUILDING ON MOMENTUM OF MILLION MAN MARCH,
LOCAL AGENCY EXTENDS REACH
IN AFRICAN-AMERICAN COMMUNITY

"MAKE 'EM ALL MARKETERS" APPROACH BRINGS
SUSTAINED DOUBLE-DIGIT BUDGET GROWTH
TO CHILD WELFARE AGENCY

**What can everyone associated with your organization do to promote the cause? A lot!**

Suggest getting involved in marketing and most people imagine the worst: *It's my nightmare. They're going to make me do solicitations.* Reassure them. There are many other ways to join in. And once they get their feet wet, some may even overcome their initial fears. Everyone can:

- Know the organization's goals and be on the lookout for sources of support

- Be a public relations ambassador and create understanding and enthusiasm for the cause

- Add names of people they know to prospect lists and open doors with personal introductions

- Invite people to attend programs and events

- Encourage friends and associates to purchase memberships, tickets, and subscriptions

- Host or make presentations at cultivation events

- Personalize requests for support via mail, telephone, E-mail, and FAX

And, with encouragement, training and support, *almost* everyone can:

- Make direct face-to-face solicitations

Asking people to participate in these efforts will be everything from surprising to exciting to off-putting. Some resistance is natural, but a thoughtful and caring effort will bring most folks along. To succeed, we have to step outside our comfort zones. Bottom line, our missions demand it.

## For those ready to ignite the power

Years ago, nonprofits turned up their noses at marketing, judging it crass and foreign to the spirit of mission-based work. Today, most realize marketing is crucial, that it helps us understand and meet the evolving needs of our many audiences, that it increases essential resources and support . . . and that it's often enjoyable.

This book provides in-depth guidance on one aspect of the marketing process—mobilizing people to participate directly in promotion campaigns. It is not a substitute for the strategic groundwork upon which such efforts succeed, nor does it take the place of comprehensive marketing planning. Regardless of the size of your organization or the scope of your marketing efforts, the ten steps in this book *can* help you:

- Systematically refine annual membership, enrollment, product sales, fund-raising, or other drives

- Plan and implement major "one-shot" initiatives such as a capital campaign or promotion for a special event

- Organize volunteer recruitment on an ongoing or short-term basis

- Analyze a target audience to determine your best prospects

- Develop key messages for use throughout your promotion efforts

- Train any size group in effective one-to-one promotional techniques
- Increase your ability to provide support, rewards, and recognition to those involved
- Develop the ability and confidence of everyone associated with your organization to be effective marketing representatives
- Increase name recognition and awareness of your organization or cause

*The focused efforts of dedicated people can make an enormous difference.*

Successful campaigns have three key ingredients: (1) a commitment to planning and action; (2) the largest possible number of "marketing representatives"; and (3) training, follow-up, and support so everyone involved can effectively play a part. It's a new spin on an old story. *People* have always been the greatest asset to nonprofit causes, and it is still the focused efforts of dedicated people that can make an enormous difference.

There is work to do to ready the organization. There is training to conduct to build skills. This book will help you do both. The key ingredient is already in place: people who care deeply about your mission, the vitality of your organization, and the impact you want to make.

## What You Will Find in This Book

There are five sections to this workbook. The first is a review of marketing principles and the planning process detailed in my first book, *Marketing Workbook for Nonprofit Organizations Volume I*. The second and third major sections, *Ready the Organization* and *Mobilize Your Marketing Representatives*, provide a ten-step, soup-to-nuts approach for developing and carrying out a people-based promotion campaign. Following those sections are four appendices—including master copies of worksheets for each step—that provide additional information and tools for your effort. Finally, one copy of the *Pocket Guide for Marketing Representatives*[1] accompanies this volume and is available in quantity as a handy reference for your marketing representatives.

Following is an overview of each of these sections.

---

[1] Marketing Workbook for Nonprofit Organizations Volume I *and additional copies of* Pocket Guide for Marketing Representatives *are available from Wilder Publishing Center, 1-800-274-6024. Additional information and an order form are at the back of this book.*

## A Review: Demystifying Marketing

A sound organizational marketing plan is the basis for mobilizing people to participate in promotion efforts. *A Review: Demystifying Marketing* will refresh your "marketing memory" and set the stage for the promotion effort to follow. Beginning on page 13, you will find a definition of marketing and a brief review of the five steps to developing a marketing plan: set marketing goals, position the organization, conduct a marketing audit, develop a marketing plan, and develop a promotion campaign.

This book builds on a thorough understanding of your overall goals, unique niche, and a "customer-friendly" operational plan that removes barriers and delivers the benefits your audiences want and need. As you go forward with mobilizing people, you will dig deeper into some aspects of marketing, while glossing over others. If you discover the need to do so, turn to *Volume I* for help resolving more comprehensive marketing planning questions.

## Phase I: Ready the Organization

Expanding the organization's involvement in marketing starts with planning the effort and preparing everyone to support it. You are embarking on a process that will likely require new practices and systems and create change for both staff and volunteers. It is necessary to lay a solid foundation that demonstrates commitment, leadership, and the ability to support each individual's contribution as a marketing representative. When you have completed this phase, you will be prepared to mobilize people and inspire confidence and enthusiasm.

*Phase I: Ready the Organization* (pages 17–63) tells you how to plan your promotion campaign in five steps. These steps are:

1. Define the scope of your effort
2. Form a Marketing Task Force
3. Set goals; define targeting, message, and communications strategies
4. Determine roles, people to involve, and recruitment techniques
5. Develop a master timeline and action plan for the effort.

A brief description of each of these five steps follows.

### Step 1: Define the scope of your effort

A variety of marketing challenges faces every nonprofit group. Based on your strategic direction and marketing plans, you may be poised to launch a major overall initiative with goals in multiple categories of resources and support. On the other hand, your present needs may be highly focused, such as a capital campaign, a membership drive, or an annual crusade to make sure gifts are under every tree on Christmas morning. In Step 1, you define the purpose of your effort, likely participants, timeline, and budget considerations.

### Step 2: Form a Marketing Task Force

The initial push for greater involvement in marketing may come from anywhere in the organization. Once a decision has been made to proceed, a Marketing Task Force should be created—or an existing group assigned—to develop and oversee the effort. The group may be relatively small—up to twelve members—and should include representatives of the major staff and volunteer groups who will later participate. The Task Force should have at least one representative from the board of directors and upper management. The executive director and, as appropriate, the board chair may certainly be Task Force members. If not, their endorsement and encouragement in other ways are critical throughout the marketing effort in order to model commitment and leadership from the top. In Step 2, you will recruit Task Force chairs and members, convene a first meeting, and prepare for next steps.

### Step 3: Set goals; define targeting, message, and communications strategies

Once the Marketing Task Force has its first meeting and is clear on overall responsibilities, it's time to dive right into the heart of the matter. Marketing goals may have already been proposed, or the Task Force may need to define them. Once goals are set, you will need to answer three strategic questions: (1) Who is your target audience? (2) What is your message? and (3) How will you communicate it? In Step 3, the Task Force will segment and prioritize your target audience; develop a case statement, a slogan or tag line, and a set of persuasive statements; and choose a mix of communications materials and techniques. At the conclusion of this step, your sights are set and you have the blueprint for a successful promotion effort.

### Step 4: Determine roles, people to involve, and recruitment techniques

In Step 4, the Task Force addresses the four major roles for marketing representatives—*Ambassador, Door-Opener, Cultivator,* and *Solicitor*—and determines which individual employees, board members, current volunteers, and friends of the organization will be tapped to participate in the promotion effort. The design of your effort may also call for new leadership roles, such as a chair or cochairs for a specific campaign. The Task Force develops mini-job descriptions for all roles and makes plans for recruiting marketing representatives.

### Step 5: Develop a master timeline and action plan for the effort

Step 5 is the final step to ready the organization. In it, the Task Force gains an overall view of the effort, then lays out next steps, identifies coordinators, sets deadlines, finalizes budgets, and otherwise puts finishing touches on the design of the promotion campaign. The Task Force sets a schedule for production of materials, outlines plans for dynamic motivational training, assigns responsibility for follow-up and support, and designs rewards and recognition for marketing representatives. With final endorsement from top management—and necessary funds—it's *look-out-world-here-we-come* as you go on to implement your plans.

## Phase II: Mobilize Your Marketing Representatives

The first hurdle when engaging people directly in marketing is a psychological one: the mere mention of it often fills their heads with scary stereotypes of used-car salesmen unscrupulously hawking their wares. Once people make the connection between marketing and a mission they respect, such concerns start to melt away. People need to understand the purpose of the effort and why their involvement is important. As you mobilize your marketing representatives, you will address fears, teach new skills, provide individual follow-up and support, and generate a *can-do!* spirit.

*Phase II: Mobilize Your Marketing Representatives* (pages 65–102) includes five steps. These are:

1. Implement the recruitment plan
2. Hold motivational training
3. Provide ongoing follow-up and support
4. Reward, recognize, reenlist
5. Celebrate success and evaluate the effort

## Step 6: Implement the recruitment plan

*Ready* . . . the Marketing Task Force has thought this through . . . *Set* . . . and outlined a recruitment plan . . . *Go!* . . . it's time to implement. Recruiting is a promotion effort in and of itself. You want to make a positive first impression and have people buy in to the plan. The recruitment plan lays out roles and responsibilities for prospective marketing representatives, stating *who* is to be approached and *how* to approach them. In Step 6, you will attend to details, produce your first promotional materials, hold a mini-training for recruiters, and have your first chance to post results. The objective: gain agreement from marketing representatives to sign on.

## Step 7: Hold motivational training

In Step 7, you'll hold motivational training sessions. While not exactly a Broadway debut, rave reviews are definitely desirable. (There *will* be critics in the audience.) Motivational training sessions may be specially planned, or they may be included on the agenda at regularly scheduled board, staff, or volunteer meetings. The sessions introduce newly engaged marketing representatives to the overall purpose behind your efforts and to their specific roles in the upcoming campaign. You will build skills, address concerns, and introduce exercises from the *Pocket Guide for Marketing Representatives*. This is the moment for confidence and enthusiasm building—it's the official launch of your marketing effort—so naturally the sessions will be upbeat, fun, and . . . motivational!

## Step 8: Provide ongoing follow-up and support

Congratulations, you're launched! Depending on how the overall effort is designed, aggressive self-starters may quickly have you running to keep up. In Step 8, the focus is tracking, coordination, and individualized support. Your marketing representatives are out in the field, each with their individual plans. You will work closely with them to update prospect lists, report progress and results, help with presentations and cultivation events, strategize on approaches to specific individuals, and send out invitations and materials. You will be on the phone and E-mail constantly with reminders, reassurance, RSVPs, and last-minute details. Your marketing representatives need backup, coaching, and fans in the bleachers cheering them on!

## Step 9: Reward, recognize, reenlist

It's not quite time to throw a *big* party (see Step 10), but well-placed balloons and streamers are more than just a nice touch along the way. In Step 9, you attend to the personal touches that keep people involved in the campaign: rewards and recognition. *Rewards* express your direct appreciation of the value and importance of other people's efforts. They range from simple and generous thank-yous to pins, pens, and post-its to giving the whole staff a Friday afternoon off. *Recognition* is more formal and more public. While your plan may include plaques or certificates for all, it's individualized gag gifts and touching tales that make recognition memorable. When it comes to *reenlistment*, timing is everything. If you're just completing an all-out campaign, most folks might need a rest. On the other hand, "striking while the iron is hot" may help you capture the momentum you've created and sign on future leaders.

## Step 10: Celebrate success and evaluate the effort

*Now* it's time to party. Whether your effort was monumental or modest, everyone who contributed along the way deserves to celebrate what you've accomplished. The main consideration in Step 10 is creating a truly enjoyable event. This is also a time when formal recognition takes place. Celebrations vary greatly, but three ingredients are essential: festivities, food, and a meaningful reminder of how you have furthered your mission. In Step 10, you will also document your results against goals and record lessons learned for the future.

# Appendices

The next section, *Appendices*, consists of helpful tips and worksheets for putting your promotion campaign into action. Here is what you'll find in each appendix:

**Appendix A: Message Testing** provides guidance on how to gain advance feedback on your key messages before you put them to use on a larger scale.

**Appendix B: Motivational Training Guides** provides detailed agendas and workshop exercises to build the understanding, skills, and commitment of your marketing representatives.

**Appendix C: Tips for Marketing Representatives** provides pointed and practical insights for everyone you've prepared to go out there and *ask*.

**Appendix D: Worksheets** provides master copies of the worksheets for the Marketing Task Force, coordinators, and others carrying out each of the workbook's ten steps.

## Pocket Guide for Marketing Representatives

This workbook comes with a companion piece called *Pocket Guide for Marketing Representatives*. In Phase II, your marketing representatives will participate in training to motivate and prepare them for their roles in the promotion effort. The Pocket Guide is a mini-workbook for use during training. It's also a ready reminder your marketing representatives can carry with them wherever they go. The Pocket Guide includes:

- An introduction to nonprofit marketing
- Motivational messages emphasizing the importance of marketing representatives and encouraging their efforts
- A mini-workbook section to accompany training, underscore marketing goals, and reinforce techniques that will help achieve them
- Space for notes, reminders, and names of key contacts in the organization who will provide follow-up and support
- Helpful tips for all marketing representatives

## How to Use This Book

*Marketing Workbook for Nonprofit Organizations Volume II* is designed as a flexible resource to help you set and achieve marketing goals. You may:

- Follow all ten steps and complete each worksheet, or select only the steps and worksheets you see as necessary
- Create a Marketing Task Force and new work groups, or assign responsibility to existing committees and teams
- Utilize current mailing lists, promotional materials, and other marketing resources you have previously developed, or create brand new ones
- Adapt the steps and processes in whatever ways are best for you

Those of you who work in **smaller organizations** are always on guard against biting off more than you can chew. This book can help focus and refine the efforts—no matter how modest—you already undertake. If you can count your current corps of marketing representatives on one hand, increasing the number of those involved by even two or three makes a big difference. If coordination of a promotion campaign looks overwhelming, then even one leadership volunteer may tip the scales in your favor. Keep the long-term benefits of enhanced outreach in mind, then commit to what you can realistically achieve at this time.

Those of you who work in **larger organizations** also have full plates. You're less likely than smaller organizations to see promotion as a one-for-all-and-all-for-one proposition. Again, this book can help you refine current campaigns and begin new ones—with the added challenge of working across organizational lines. Start with the top of the organization. Follow-through on the total effort means organizational leaders have to champion a philosophy of involvement, make a visible commitment as role models, and ensure necessary time and resources throughout the organization to achieve results.

Whether large or small, you can mobilize people for marketing success when you have:

- Set clear marketing goals
- Ensured high-quality products and services
- Made a commitment and readied the organization to implement promotion efforts
- Recruited, trained, and prepared to support your marketing representatives
- Set a date to celebrate results

> This workbook is a guide, but you're in charge of the trip.

## Get familiar

This workbook is a guide, but you're in charge of the trip! As you chart your own course, it will be helpful to study introductory portions and page ahead through the whole workbook to familiarize yourself with all aspects of the material.

## Make plenty of worksheets

Master worksheets are provided for each of the ten steps. Please feel free to make as many copies as you like and save the originals for future use.

## Utilize database systems

Your promotion effort is bound to include lists and contact information for a great many people. A number of software packages are readily available to help keep input, tracking, and updating to a minimum. Consider how you can adapt worksheets and lists to database systems and, when more efficient, bypass paper altogether.

## Include the right people

Each step includes a suggested list of participants for that step. Some will be with you from start to finish and take multiple roles, while others briefly enter and exit at particular points. Think broadly about who to involve from inside your organization and be sure to gain the input of outside specialists whenever needed.

## Keep it moving

This is an action book. It's about defining important results and achieving them. From the very start, you will be mobilizing people and—as in any group—there are some who want detailed plans before making a move and others eager to start yesterday. Find the most comfortable pace for you and be prepared: when you're on the right track with marketing, things snowball fast.

## Have a marketing mind

True marketers know what they have to offer, listen intently to what others value, and are passionate about delivering the goods.

*"He's a born marketer."* People described this way—whether he or she— believe in possibilities, view the world as a place of abundance, and know there is always a place in people's lives for right and important things. "Nothing ventured, nothing gained" are bywords. Opportunity knocks constantly. True marketers know what they have to offer, listen intently to what others value, and are passionate about delivering the goods.

• • •

As you move through your effort, remember the spirit of Mae West who said, "One and one makes two, and two and two makes four, and four and four makes ten if you know how to work it right."

Now *that's* a marketing mind.

# Demystifying Marketing

Marketing is an age-old practice. It involves two parties agreeing to a mutually beneficial exchange. The definition of marketing for nonprofits is: *a process that helps you exchange something of value for something you need.* It is a *process* because it takes time to conduct research, develop marketing plans, carry them out, and achieve results. The goal is to create *exchange relationships*—the kind we participate in as consumers all the time. We pay a fair price for something we want. We spend time at a free seminar or support group because we benefit from it. We commit our time as volunteers and gain the satisfaction of doing good for others. We make these exchanges because we get something we *value*, as does the individual or organization on the other side.

Marketing:
a process that helps
you exchange
something of value for
something you need.

Looking back, we can see few cases in which we leapt out of bed in the morning, suddenly motivated to attend that benefit auction, join that alumni group, or map out a delivery route for Meals on Wheels. Chances are we were targeted by someone's marketing plan, possibly cultivated over time, and maybe even received a personal invitation from someone we knew. Once we were ready to take a first step, other matters of convenience, cost, and customer service had to fall into place. And when we finally made a decision and spent our money or time, the experience we had in that exchange relationship either set us on the road to being a satisfied customer or led to a disappointing dead end.

To achieve their ultimate aim—satisfying and even delighting customers—the most effective marketing efforts are thought through from beginning to end. In *Marketing Workbook for Nonprofit Organizations Volume I*, I map out five steps that help nonprofits develop and implement successful marketing plans. Following is a review of those steps.

*To define the results you want and provide focus for your planning:*
## Set Marketing Goals

These are the precise, measurable results you are after, in numbers and at specific points in time; for example, 150 new members by December 31; 500 tickets sold to a concert; $25,000 raised from individual donors by June 30.

*To distinguish your organization and programs with your audiences and create the reputation you want:*
## Position the Organization

When you position your organization, you:

* Define your niche with a positioning statement; for example: *Mothers Against Drunk Driving: Crusaders for stronger action against the crime of drunk driving and the leading victim assistance organization in the nation.*

* Build recognition for your unique role with key audiences, through consistent use of slogans and other reputation-building strategies, and—most important—by delivering superior value to your customers in line with your positioning claim.

The most effective marketing efforts are thought through from beginning to end.

*To identify marketing strengths and weaknesses:*
## Conduct a Marketing Audit

In a marketing audit, you systematically uncover the answers to a number of questions, as follows:

* *Product.* Are your programs and services easy to understand and use, and of high quality?

* *Publics.* Who are your priority target audiences—the individuals and groups who can make exchanges with you that will enable you to meet your goals? Do your products deliver what they value?

* *Price.* Do your products cost too much—in money or time? Do your prices reflect the value of your products to your target audiences? Do you "underprice"—that is, set a low price when people would willingly pay more if asked?

* *Place.* Is it convenient to get what you offer? Are your locations welcoming and accessible? Do you make your product easy to obtain through customer-oriented distribution strategies?

* *Production.* Can you meet greater demand without sacrificing quality? Do you provide timely and courteous customer service?

* *Promotion.* Do you communicate with your target audiences frequently, with an appealing image, and with messages that point out the benefits they stand to gain? Do you ask people to take a specific next step?

*To map out the action necessary to achieve your goals:*

# Develop a Marketing Plan

- Conduct any necessary research to answer questions that arise from the marketing audit.

- Create a blueprint that defines your product, targets your audiences, sets your price, place, and production strategies, and outlines your promotion plan.

- Develop a timeline and action plan to bring the blueprint to reality with major steps, responsibilities, deadlines, and associated budgets.

*To choose your promotion techniques, develop necessary materials, and plan how you will deliver your message:*

# Develop a Promotion Campaign

- Use your goals, positioning statement, and marketing plan to define the creative challenges of the campaign.

- Define your image; for example, "Latino teenagers will call this a cool place to hang out"; "Concert-goers will describe the orchestra as *exciting*"; "Wage-earning women will see us as relevant."

- Work with marketing communications professionals to create key messages, choose techniques, and develop all aspects of the promotion campaign.

- Recruit, train, and support everyone associated with the organization to be effective marketing representatives.

Marketing is results-oriented and every marketing plan should be evaluated. The standard is whether or not you achieve your goals. If you do achieve them, it means the plan is sound and, with fine-tuning, your approach bears repeating. If you fall short, it is necessary to repeat the planning process with an eye to uncovering and correcting miscalculations or missteps.

My first strategic planning mentor passed along the following wisdom: *Organizations that develop and implement strategic plans routinely outperform those that don't.* The same applies to marketing. All nonprofits do marketing, but the organization that develops and implements comprehensive plans is still the exception. The steps in this volume go into depth on targeting publics, developing key messages, and carrying out a powerful promotion campaign. This book *does not* address fundamental questions on the essential match between the wants, needs, and aspirations of your audiences and the products you offer. For promotion campaigns to be on solid ground, everything about your organization must be "customer-friendly" and your products must deliver *value*. If you need to address these issues, take time to do so before embarking on a large-scale promotion campaign.

> Everything about your organization must be "customer-friendly" and your products must deliver *value*.

Marketing is routine to daily life. Constant targets of others' campaigns, we scarcely give it a second thought. When marketers ourselves, we need to dive in and attend to a progression of gritty details. It all stems from the single idea of *mutually satisfying exchanges*. When we have something of value and want to exchange it for something we need, then we must state what we're after, know who can give it to us, be prepared to deliver what *they* value, and craft our campaign to reach out.

Far from a mystery, marketing is a common practice based on common sense. With dutiful planning, persistence, and broad participation, the payoff—increased resources and support—is a handsome one.

*"Strategy begins with the mission. It leads to a work plan. It ends with the right tools, a kit, say for volunteers, which tells them who to call on, what to say, and how much money to get. Without that kit, there is no strategy."* [2]

— Peter F. Drucker

**PHASE I**

# *Ready the Organization*

In Phase I you lay a solid foundation for your promotion campaign. You will build commitment and develop action plans crucial to success. The five steps of Phase I are:

[2] *From* Managing the Non-Profit Organization *by Peter F. Drucker, copyright 1990, HarperCollins, New York City.*

DEFINE THE SCOPE OF YOUR EFFORT

# Define the Scope of Your Effort

The effort you are about to undertake has a fresh twist: many more people will be involved in your outreach efforts. For some organizations, this is a natural extension of what is currently in place. For others, this is an opportunity to pilot a whole new approach.

To flesh out a promotion campaign, you will need a concise statement that answers the question "How big and for what?" Organizations reach this jumping-off point by different routes. Comprehensive planning may have already determined the scope of your effort. Perhaps urgent needs came up suddenly and you've got to act now. Or you might simply feel there is a need to do *something* and it's time to decide exactly what.

## Scope is defined by purpose, participants, timeline, and budget

*Scope* means something aimed at or desired, what one wishes to effect, an overall purpose or end. To define the scope of your effort, you will address *purpose, participants, timeline,* and *budget.* Completing this step provides an official charge to an existing committee or team or a specially created Marketing Task Force.

The idea for a people-to-people promotion campaign might originate with any individual or group, but the scope and commitment to proceed must come from the top leadership of your organization. In most cases this means approval from the executive director. The board of directors should be informed and, when appropriate, should be asked to formally endorse the concept.

In the following case study, a start-up nursery school defined its scope *and* met its enrollment goals—all within five months:

### From Zero to Sixty in Five Months

A synagogue nursery school is launching *Yom HaShemesh* (Sunny Day), its first summer program offered as part of an expansion of services to meet needs for year-round child care. To make a go of it, *Yom HaShemesh* needs sixty children registered. Two parents who helped plan the program step forward and volunteer to lead a promotion effort. The scope of the effort is confirmed in a meeting with the nursery school director, the two key volunteers, the chair of the Nursery School Committee, and a few other active school parents.

The purpose and goal are already clear, as is the need for major outreach beyond the usual minimal announcements that appear in the *Temple Bulletin*. Current volunteers, teachers, and the synagogue's rabbis, staff, and board of trustees are to be tapped as marketing representatives. The timeline looks pretty short—there are just five months until opening day, and, at this point, barely anyone even knows about the new summer program.

A raft of new materials and money for community newspaper inserts are needed. The budget becomes the immediate issue—money for promotions isn't in it. Not enough can be built into program fees, so the two lead volunteers—now cochairs of the Marketing Task Force—fast-track a process through the synagogue hierarchy and obtain two small, but sufficient, internal grants.

By the end of three months there are over fifty marketing representatives talking up the program. Teachers and volunteers pass out materials and chat up parents during drop-off and pick-up times; the head rabbi makes announcements during Friday evening services; flyers are printed and distributed to the whole congregation, to surrounding neighborhoods, and through a Jewish newspaper; and volunteers make enough promotional and follow-up phone calls to joke about starting a telemarketing firm. Two months later the program opens to fifty-eight children—close enough—and a potluck picnic is scheduled to celebrate success and hand out "You are my sunshine" recognition certificates.

**Who to involve in this step:**

*Those with vision and energy for a new promotion effort. The executive director and board representatives should participate and officially endorse the scope and next steps.*

# 1. Clarify Purpose

Your intentions may be laser-like or sweeping, depending on your organization's circumstances, needs, and opportunities. For example:

- The long-term strategic plan calls for community-wide capital and membership drives.

- Operating support has leveled off or gone into decline and it's time to cultivate new grassroots sources of funding.

- A serious situation—declining enrollment, sudden loss of support, unacceptably low season ticket sales—requires rallying the troops for immediate short-term action.

- Opportunities abound and your immediate need is for more people ready and able to pursue them.

To clarify the purpose of your new promotion effort, turn to Worksheet 1, Section 1 (page 135) and address three issues:

A. The situation or need that your promotion effort will address

B. What types of resources, support, or response the effort will produce

C. How the organization's capabilities or skills will be enhanced

> Anyone associated with your organization can be an excellent marketing representative.

# 2. Identify Groups of Potential Marketing Representatives

For small organizations, who to recruit as marketing representatives may be easy to decide: everyone! Larger groups have greater choices. At this point, you don't need to list people by name or know their exact roles, just the major groups to include. Thinking through this question should start with *who will be approached*—your likely pool of participants. Anyone associated with your organization can be an excellent marketing representative. Staff participation may be strongly encouraged, even mandatory. Board members, volunteers, and friends of the organization should all be considered. Concerns of those you recruit will include "How much time will this take?" and "What exactly will I be doing?" You'll probably hear discomfort with the idea of face-to-face solicitation. The steps you are just starting to work through will prepare you to offer four marketing representative roles, each with a different level of commitment and intensity.

Now turn to Worksheet 1, Section 2A (page 136) to identify potential groups of marketing representatives.

In addition to determining potential participant groups, you must decide who will be asked to take leadership roles by serving on a Marketing Task Force. The Task Force's mission is *to plan, help implement, and evaluate a people-to-people promotion campaign.* The group should be relatively small; up to twelve people is best. Here are guidelines to use in identifying potential members. The Task Force should include:

- At least one person who helped define the scope of the effort (this step)

- Representatives from groups who will later be asked to participate

- Individuals with a strong understanding of marketing, communications, and direct solicitation in a nonprofit environment

- One or more board representatives

- An upper management representative

- Others who can help move the effort forward

- A potential chair or cochairs

While executive director input is necessary to the Task Force, it is not essential that he or she be a full member.

To identify potential participants, go to Worksheet 1, Section 2B (page 137).

## 3. Set an Overall Timeline

Time may or may not be on your side. If your new marketing effort is driven by pressing needs, deadlines aren't optional. If the situation allows more leeway, then develop your timeline in light of other priorities for staff and volunteers and the real time it may take to accomplish your purpose. "We should have started weeks ago!" is a common refrain of groups coming to grips with the details of their effort. There are people to recruit, materials to design, training and systems to put in place . . . do your best to strike a balance in your timeline that puts the entire effort into view—from inception to celebration—but allows you to "fast-forward" in whatever ways necessary. The steps in this book are designed to support efforts ranging from the short-term push to the multiyear campaign.

To set your timeline, turn to Worksheet 1, Section 3 (page 138).

# 4. Address Budget Issues

In the example of the synagogue nursery school on page 20, it was possible to project costs while determining the scope of the effort. You may be able to set a budget at this point, whether based on history with past efforts or because you have enough information in front of you to make good estimates. If not, subsequent steps in Ready the Organization will help you build a budget.

By the same token, you may already have money set aside, know where you will get it, or need to make plans for funding the effort.

To address budget issues, turn to Worksheet 1, Section 4 (page 140) and answer three questions:

   A. What is your ballpark budget for the promotion effort?

   • Do you have an estimate now?

   • Will you build an estimate as you go along?

   B. What funds are already secured?

   C. What is your plan for securing additional funds?

FORM A MARKETING TASK FORCE

# Form a Marketing Task Force

A Marketing Task Force will play a primary role throughout your promotion effort. The group will set or affirm goals, develop and help implement plans, and evaluate results. In this step, you will complete a charge statement for the Task Force, recruit members and a chair or cochairs, and convene a first meeting.

**Who to involve in this step:**

*A subset of those who determined the scope (Step 1), the executive director and board chair or their delegates, and the Task Force chair or cochairs.*

## 1. Complete the Task Force Charge Statement

The mission of the Task Force is *to plan, help implement, and evaluate a people-to-people promotion campaign.* To do this work, the Task Force needs to be guided by a *charge statement*. The charge statement should have the following elements:

A. The purpose of the promotion effort; and—if they are already set— the goals of the effort

B. Groups expected to participate

C. An overall timeline with check-in points

D. A budget or expectations to create one; sources of funds or a funding plan

E. Parameters that specify any absolute "dos" or "don'ts"

F. A "point person" or group to whom the Task Force is responsible

Points A–D on the previous page can be summarized from Worksheet 1. For Point E, include information to keep the Task Force mindful of important organizational issues. "Dos" might include honoring your diversity plans throughout the effort, checking a master calendar before scheduling meetings or events, or inviting particular people to play a role. "Don'ts" could be particular people or groups *not* to target or include, budgets that may not be dipped into, or certain time periods that are already booked for other purposes.

Turn to Worksheet 2, Section 1 (page 141) to complete your charge statement.

## 2.  Recruit a Chair or Cochairs

Many individuals will have leadership positions throughout the marketing effort—some as guest stars, others in long-term principal roles. The key qualification for chairs is the ability to lead the Task Force to a successful completion of its mission. A range of skills makes someone the "right person"; but, above all, the chair or cochairs should have drive and enthusiasm for the job. Before rounding up the usual suspects, think about who might enjoy the opportunity. Also consider the creative potential of a shared leadership role. Prime movers on the project so far may be strong considerations. It is helpful to have a "B-list" of candidates should your first choices be unable or unwilling to accept the responsibility.

To underscore organizational commitment to the marketing effort and the importance of the leadership role, the executive director or board chair should meet with prospective Task Force chairs, explain the scope and charge, extend the invitation, and gain acceptance.

Go to Worksheet 2, Part 2A (page 143) to identify Task Force chairs, and then go on to recruit them.

## 3.  Recruit Task Force Members

Once Task Force chairs are in place, they will help invite other Task Force members to sign on. At this point:

A. The list of prospective members from Worksheet 1, Section 2B, is discussed and possibly amended.

B. Possible dates for a first meeting are set.

C. The point person and Task Force chair determine who is best suited to talk with each prospective member to extend the invitation, explain the purpose of the Task Force, gain acceptance, and poll for availability to attend a first meeting.

Turn to Worksheet 2, Section 2B (page 143) to prepare to recruit Task Force members, and then go on to do so.

# 4. Convene a First Meeting

The first Task Force meeting should be carefully planned to ensure a well-organized and positive start to the group's work. Task Force members should prepare by reading the introductory sections of this workbook and the portion of Step 3, Set Goals, that deals with setting or affirming marketing goals (pages 30–33). If they are not designated members of the Task Force, the point person, executive director, or board chair should attend the first meeting to help underscore the importance of the effort. This meeting marks the passing of the baton from those who did the initial planning to the leadership group that carries out the effort.

## Suggested first meeting agenda

Use the following agenda as the guide for your Task Force's first meeting. As there is a great deal to cover, this first meeting should be scheduled to last three hours.

1. In addition to straightforward introductions, ask each member to briefly describe his or her "best marketing experience"—on either side of an exchange relationship.

2. Determine how note taking and note distribution will happen. Identify a note taker for this meeting.

3. Ask what questions or concerns people would like addressed in the meeting.

4. Briefly discuss the Task Force mission and charge statements to ensure that everyone understands and agrees with them.

5. Briefly preview the next steps to Ready the Organization.

6. Briefly discuss marketing goals. Ensure everyone understands that goals for your effort need to be expressed as specific numerical results to be achieved by a particular deadline.

7. Determine what information the Task Force will need to be able to set or affirm goals at the next meeting.

8. Determine next steps and who is responsible to carry them out.

9. Set an initial calendar of meetings.

10. Respond to questions or issues raised that have not already been addressed.

11. Note discussion items to be carried over to future meetings.

12. Additional items.

It is now time to convene your first Task Force meeting.

SET GOALS; DEFINE TARGETING, MESSAGE, AND COMMUNICATIONS STRATEGIES

# Set Goals; Define Targeting, Message, and Communications Strategies

Think back for a moment to the definition of marketing and the central word *exchange*. In your marketing effort, you will seek many exchanges to gain what your organization needs, whether it be funds, volunteers, program participation, or other categories of resources and support. Once the Marketing Task Force has held its organizational meeting, the first order of business is to zero in on the exchanges you want (marketing goals), as well as three critical marketing strategies—targeting, key messages, and communications.

- **Marketing goals**: what you want, how much, and by when
- **Targeting**: the prioritized groups of people you will approach to make exchanges
- **Key messages**: what you will show and tell to create understanding and motivate people to respond
- **Communications:** the materials and techniques you will use to convey key messages

**Who to involve in this step:**

*The Marketing Task Force and, if desired, a facilitator or consultant.*

## 1. Set or Affirm Marketing Goals
*Create specific, measurable goals that drive planning and action*

Marketing goals are specific and measurable. They set the direction for both planning and action, and they provide benchmarks for evaluation. Here are examples:

- Raise $25,000 in individual contributions by December 31
- Obtain $50 million in capital pledges to the Building Our Future Fund within five years
- Recruit 150 new volunteers for Make a Difference Day by August 15
- Receive 500 applications for admission by April 1
- Sign up 25 businesses for the in-kind materials network within one year
- Draw a total of 30 people to block club organizing meetings on March 2 and 3
- Gain 1,000 membership renewals and 100 new members by June 30

The Task Force is likely facing one of three scenarios as it prepares to set goals:

1. The purpose of the effort sets direction, but not specific goals.
   *"We know what we want. We just don't know how much is possible . . . ."*

2. Goals are already fully defined through a broader marketing planning process, through formal contractual commitments, or by a crisis situation.
   *"We know what we need—let's get after it!"*

3. Goals are wide open.
   *"Since this is a pilot project, let's get a group together and empower them to design the whole thing."*

Whether or not marketing goals were preset for the Task Force as a part of its initial charge, it is important to review desired results, affirm them, or, as in the following case example, insist they be revised.

**Tilting at Windmills**

In the course of its strategic planning process, a midsized organization focused on revitalization of low-income neighborhoods sets an annual fund-raising goal of $200,000 (up from $50,000) to be reached in one year and maintained thereafter. The group has a solid financial base with government contracts and a few steady corporate grants, but is ambitious and believes the additional $150,000 is out there.

A volunteer Task Force is formed with a go-getter board member as chair. At first, the goal is taken for granted; it's just a matter of how it will happen. But as the Task Force gets into targeting and tries to determine reasonable expectations of each segment, the numbers don't add up. On top of that, a heated debate breaks out over the issue of asking low-income clients to contribute.

The chair feels caught between goals he agreed to accomplish and what the group sees as possible, while the executive director is getting worried about a group of eager volunteers feeling rushed through important issues. One Task Force member turns the tide when she says, "I don't mind a big challenge, but I didn't sign up for the Impossible Dream Team! This isn't do-or-die, so let's slow down and get it right." The chair realizes he would rather help establish a positive track record than charge off tilting at windmills. He agrees to put himself on the line with the board and argue that goals for the first two years need to be substantially reduced, even if it means a revision of the strategic plan.

Great care needs to be taken in goal setting. You will be involving many people on your "Dream Team" and their sense of achievement is at stake. But don't err too far on the side of caution, either. Many groups exceed even highly ambitious goals and some continuously suffer from setting their sights too low. Goals should be realistic and achievable, especially if this will be your marketing representatives' first time out.

Most nonprofit marketing goals fall into the categories of:

- Funding
- Volunteer recruiters
- Participation in programs, services, or events
- Enrollment
- Membership
- Sales of tickets, books, services, or other items
- In-kind contributions

You may wish to pursue a single result for this effort or to address goals in multiple categories, depending on the overall marketing plans and capacity of the organization. A marketing rule of thumb is to maximize opportunities for response from any audience or prospect. This may mean targeting certain groups for multiple goals; for example, you may ask the same person to purchase season tickets, reserve a spot for the opening gala, and make an annual contribution.

To begin, each individual goal category should be addressed separately. To set or affirm goals, you will respond to four questions, discussed below. The result will be a draft decision to guide the development of targeting, key message, and communications strategies that correspond to each goal. At the end of Step 3, you will return to these draft goals to confirm or revise them.

### 1. What are the ideal results we could achieve in our effort?

The purpose for your overall effort defines one or more categories for marketing goals. First, determine your categories. Then take the opportunity to think big within each one. If everything fell into place, how much response—in measurable numbers—could you generate? Blue skies and a little dreaming are fine at this point. The discussion points that follow are designed to pull the Task Force down to earth.

### 2. What argues in favor of our ability to achieve these ideal results?

Your organization's track record is a good place to start. Is there a solid foundation to build on? Do you believe you've fully tapped the prospects you know are out there? Is there a crisis, a sense of urgency, or momentum to spur you on? Is there high demand for what you offer? Does your mission deal with popular issues? Are trends favorable? Discuss what seems possible inside the organization and in the community.

### 3. What argues against our ability to achieve these results?

Take a second look at your track record. How good is it, really? Does the organization want this badly enough to go after it 100 percent? Are you known and respected where it counts? Do people easily "get" and agree with the importance of what you do? How stiff is the competition? Are trends unfavorable? Take a hard look and don't be afraid to raise difficult issues or touch on worst-case scenarios.

A marketing rule of thumb is to maximize opportunities for response from any audience or prospect.

## 4. What are our realistic, achievable goals? By when?

Take a little time for reflection on what you've just discussed. Then go through each goal category and poll the group for each individual's gut response. If you are affirming preset goals, ask if they are too ambitious, not ambitious enough, or fine as they are. If you are setting new goals, ask for specific amounts, deadlines, and brief comments. Next, take a look at the range of responses and discuss them. What is realistic and achievable? Is everyone willing to agree to a draft decision? (For example, 115 participants in children's drama workshops by June 1.) If you can't reach a general consensus, state your goal as a low-end to high-end range (for example, 100 to 125 participants in children's drama workshops by June 1) and proceed from there.

You will find the goal-setting questions on Worksheet 3, Section 1 (page 145).

# 2. Set Targeting Strategy
### *Prioritize the market segments you will approach to make exchanges*

Now that you have a well-developed idea of what you want, you must decide who to go after to get it. Many people start by saying, "The public is our audience." However, from a marketing perspective, there is no such thing as "the public." There are only individual *segments* of the public that add up to a whole. Some of these segments make great prospects to approach. Targeting others would put your marketing representatives on a wild goose chase. Those with *the capacity to make exchanges you want* or those who are *most desirable to reach* define your target audiences.

Imagine a real target—the kind you aim at on an archery range. When you set targeting strategy, you begin by listing all the groups that could fit anywhere on the target. Then you decide which groups fit into the bull's-eye, which groups fit in the circle closest to the bull's-eye, which fit in the next circle, and so on. *To target* means to aim. When you have completed this exercise, you will see who to aim at in the promotion effort. This is where the prize potential lies.

### Segment your target audience into distinct groups

Segmentation needs to be done as a separate exercise for each of your marketing goals. For each goal, you begin by brainstorming a list of all groups (or individuals) who might be part of your target audience. Then you screen the list against four criteria (described at the top of page 35) and eliminate any groups that do not meet at least one.

A segment is any size group that is best approached in a unique way. It is as small as one person and almost any size from there. Characteristics that may, in combination, define a segment are:

- Current or past relationship with the organization, one of its programs, or someone associated with the organization
- A particular stake in the success of the organization or one of its programs
- Language or primary means of communication
- Race, ethnic, or cultural group
- Physical disability
- Gender identification
- Sexual orientation
- Living with serious and persistent health conditions
- Age
- Single or living with a partner; family status
- Religious or spiritual affiliation
- Place of geographic origin or common geographic boundary
- Economic status
- Level of formal education
- Values, motivations, or political leanings
- Lifestyle, profession, or interests
- Other

Examples of segments are:

- Board members (segmented by *current relationship* with the organization)
- African-American male professionals (segmented by *race, gender,* and *economic status*)
- Families with adopted children (segmented by *family status*)
- Sign-language using baby-boomer lesbians (segmented by *language, age, gender,* and *sexual orientation)*
- Wealthy alumni (segmented by *economic status* and *past relationship)*
- Area foundations and corporations (segmented by *economic status, interests,* and *geography)*
- Women living with Alzheimer's (segmented by *gender, age,* and *serious and persistent health condition)*
- "Professional philanthropists" (segmented by *values, economic status,* and *interests)*
- High school science teachers (segmented by *profession)*

Turn to Worksheet 3, Section 2A (page 148) and brainstorm as many potential market segments as you can. Then go on to test the groups on your list against the following four criteria and eliminate any that do not meet at least one:

- People in this segment have the capacity to make exchanges in line with your goal.
- Making exchanges with the people in the segment is desirable to your organization.
- People in this segment stand to benefit from the success of your organization or one of its programs.
- People in this segment may have an interest in your organization or a desire to make exchanges with it.

## Prioritize the segments

Now that you have segmented the target audience, you can prioritize the segments into an A-list, B-list, and C-list by rating them on three factors:

- **Capacity:** how much of what you want the segment could produce
- **Desirability:** how attractive or necessary it is to have a particular segment on board
- **Difficulty:** how much time, effort, and money are required to successfully reach a segment

### Capacity

To rate capacity, begin with your assumptions about each segment. What portion of your overall goal could each segment produce? Who could produce the most? The best predictor of future performance is past performance. You may have identified some large and promising segments, but, if you have little or no existing relationship with them, their immediate capacity may be lower than sheer numbers suggest. An excellent source of information on capacity is in the room: the knowledge and insight of Task Force members. If you need additional information to validate assumptions, you may turn to:

- Records of your own history with any given segment
- Existing demographic research and others' experience with various segments
- Primary market research in the form of interviews, surveys, or focus groups
- The opinions of expert analysts or wise observers
- A full-scale feasibility study

### Desirability

Some segments have high capacity *and* are highly desirable. They are your top priorities. Some segments have low capacity but are nevertheless highly desirable. It may seem odd for a segment with low capacity to still be highly desirable, but there are groups who, though not likely to yield a great deal themselves, remain anywhere from very attractive to absolutely necessary:

- *Opinion leaders* such as spiritual leaders, community leaders, celebrities, media professionals, and other large "grapes" on the grapevine

- *Gatekeepers* such as referral sources or potential partner organizations, government officials, key organizational decision makers, networking groups, and people known for their professional influence or social finesse

- *Mission targets* such as people of diverse backgrounds, difficult-to-reach client populations, grassroots community members, the historically disenfranchised, and others your mission and values direct you to include

As you rate each segment and assign it to the A-, B-, or C-list, consider both capacity and desirability. Rate the segments as having *high* capacity or desirability, or *low* capacity or desirability.

### Difficulty

Now that you're getting a gauge on whom you'd like to dance with, it's time to assess just how hard it might be to get them out on the floor. This time, you will rate your segments *high:* difficult to reach; or *low:* relatively easy to reach.

Those with *high difficulty* to reach may:

- Have no past experience with your organization or anyone associated with it

- Perceive little or no benefit from making exchanges with you

- Be notorious for not reading mail, failing to return phone calls, missing appointments, or being otherwise inaccessible

- Be extremely busy

- Have to be visited where they live or hang out—which may change frequently

- Expect red-carpet treatment

- Pose communications or cultural challenges to your organization

- Be approached by competing interests quite frequently

- Require expensive materials or communications techniques

- Be angry at or suspicious of you

Those with *low difficulty* to reach may:

- Have significant positive experience with your organization or people associated with it
- Perceive great benefit from making exchanges with you
- Be noteworthy for always reading mail, returning phone calls, keeping appointments, and otherwise being accessible
- Be known for making room in their schedules when it's something important
- Be people who you see on a regular basis, who are easy to bring together, or who can be reached at meetings that are already planned
- Be undemanding
- Be people whose language, communication style, and culture match yours
- Be approached by competing interests only infrequently
- Respond to inexpensive materials and communications techniques
- Love your organization and believe in its mission

Now you are ready to rate your market segments using the following formula:

$$\frac{\text{Capacity or desirability}}{\text{Difficulty}} = \text{Rating}$$

It is possible to get one of four ratings:

| **Capacity or desirability:** | High | High | Low | Low |
|---|---|---|---|---|
| **Difficulty:** | Low | High | Low | High |

As you complete your ratings, you can mark each segment for the:

| **A-list** | | **B-list** | or | **C-list** |
|---|---|---|---|---|
| High | High | Low | | Low |
| Low | High | Low | | High |

## The A-list

A High/Low segment goes on the A-list and is always a delight to find there. It means you can reach important and productive segments with minimum difficulty.

The High/High segment also belongs on the A-list and means you've got your work cut out for you. You're going to have to reach across barriers and you may face a lengthy timeline or significant promotion costs.

### The B-list

A Low/Low segment goes on the B-list. While there may not be tremendous return from B-list segments, targeting them won't cost you much, so why not? Plus, you never know—more than one low-profile segment has showered a nonprofit with unexpected gifts.

### The C-list

A Low/High segment belongs on the C-list. This is where you draw the line. You might screen in a sentimental favorite now and then, but promotion is about cost-effective results and the C-list doesn't have what it takes.

The following case example describes the strategy that grew out of one group's determination to find a way to reach its A-list.

---

## Segmentation Builds Bridges, Brings Results

AMICUS, an organization that connects inmates with volunteer friends outside of prison, has set ambitious goals to increase its corps of African Americans participating as monthly prison visitors. The target audience is easy to segment (in terms of the A-list), but mostly rates High/High (highly desirable but difficult to reach).

The characteristics of this segment are African Americans between the ages of thirty and fifty-five who are probably connected to a church, mosque, or civic organization, or who are in the legal, criminal justice, or helping professions; plus a small group labeled "out-of-the-woodwork altruists." A great difficulty is the program's identification as a "white" organization and, in fact, AMICUS has limited prospects for recruiting any sizable number of marketing representatives in the black community. For help, AMICUS' Marketing Task Force turns to a well-connected African-American board member, who agrees to host two luncheon discussions at his downtown law office with a number of community gatekeepers.

A case statement is presented and quickly endorsed by attendees, and talk turns to how successful promotion of the volunteer program might happen. Many ideas surface, including a collaborative relationship with the area Urban Coalition, whose president attends one of the luncheon discussions. At the discussion he reports a large number of inquiries from both inmates and community members about exactly the kinds of services AMICUS provides, which his organization does not. Negotiations begin with the idea of the Urban Coalition combining its extensive network of contacts with AMICUS' ability to coordinate and follow up on leads. Grant applications are written to jointly create *Rafiki* (Swahili for friend).

Following the 1995 Million Man March, the partnership catches fire. Within weeks, a major news conference features African-American leaders calling for massive community response to black inmates waiting for positive outside connections. Funders jump on board and quick results follow as the Urban Coalition's peer-to-peer network and AMICUS' new community-based outreach workers join hands to recruit new African-American volunteers.

Now, return to the list of market segments you generated on Worksheet 3, Section 2A (page 148), recopy your final list, and turn to Worksheet 3, Section 2B (page 150) to:

- Estimate how much each segment could produce

- Rate them with the formula, $\dfrac{\text{Capacity or desirability}}{\text{Difficulty}}$

- Prioritize your market segments into A-, B-, and C-lists

- Come to final consensus on your marketing goals

- Note where individual segments appear on the A- or B-lists for more than one goal

## 3. Set Key Message Strategy
### *Create interest and gain response with persuasive messages*

Now that it has segmented and prioritized the organization's audiences, the Task Force turns its attention to what the marketing representatives will *say* to engage those individuals and groups. The development of persuasive messages is an art requiring both discipline and creativity. There is a role for all Task Force members—to provide raw content—and a writing/editing role for a communications specialist. (Graphic design and the like come later.) Some key messages will be effective with all target audiences, while some audiences require highly specialized messages. The message development process goes like this:

1. Set criteria for effectiveness

2. Develop factual content

3. Identify points of resistance and receptivity

4. Develop emotional content

5. Draft key messages

6. Amend and approve messages

### 1. Set criteria for effectiveness

Decision making in creative processes can be a nightmare. Issues get hashed and rehashed until exhausted participants come to feel like so many cooks spoiling the broth. The solution is to predefine your taste test: develop a set of criteria that Task Force members can apply objectively to determine if key messages have the right ingredients.

To set criteria, first simply pose the question, "What criteria will we use to decide if the messages we create are effective?" Answers tend to come easily—we all know what grabs our attention and what doesn't. Responses can address both form and content. For example:

- Short and to the point
- Tells what we do
- Memorable, catchy
- Shows how we're unique
- Is in the language and style of our target audience

Sometimes criteria will be paradoxical, which is fine. Groups may say:

- Builds on the past/shows new direction
- Answers questions/makes people curious

There is one criterion that must be embedded in any promotional message for it to be effective:

- *Tells people what we want them to **think, feel,** and **do.***

Your key messages should *always* meet that standard.

To set additional criteria, turn to Worksheet 3, Section 3A (page 152). Once this step is finished, put the completed list aside for later use.

## 2. Develop factual content

To develop factual content for key messages, the Task Force answers these questions in light of the purpose of your promotion effort:

- What needs of our target audience do we address?
- Why is what we do important to them?
- How can we describe what we do so it's easy for others to understand?
- Who benefits from what we do and how do they benefit?
- What do we want people to think, feel, and do?

Most nonprofits have existing information and materials full of factual content. The Task Force can make its job easier by reviewing these materials in advance and pulling out useful pieces. Then information gaps can be identified and any necessary research conducted to fill them.

To develop factual content, turn to Worksheet 3, Section 3B (page 153).

· · · · · · · · · ·

Key messages should always tell people what you want them to *think, feel,* and *do.*

· · · · · · · · · ·

## 3. Identify points of resistance and receptivity

Having a strong case is one thing. The mood and perceptions of your audience are another. Knowing what pockets of resistance exist will help you craft messages designed to overcome negative perceptions. And, of course, an eye to fertile ground will help you capitalize on folks' sunny disposition.

### Identify resistance

We're usually well aware of the problems out there. The media endlessly document the public's sour mood and we know from personal experience that even people we thought sure to "get it" often don't. To help frame the message for the target audience, the Task Force should—without defensiveness or glossing over anything—list its awareness of:

- Inaccurate perceptions of the organization, its programs, or the general field of work in which the organization is involved

- Negative associations with the organization, its programs, or the general field of work

- Hostile or antagonistic attitudes

- Uninformed or negative assumptions

- Any ways in which the organization's image is tarnished

- A very crowded marketplace or "compassion fatigue" on the part of your target audience

To identify areas of resistance, go to Worksheet 3, Section 3C (page 154).

### Identify receptivity

Now for a walk down easy street. There are always the receptive few, and sometimes eager crowds, waiting to hear just what you've got to say. Maybe the planets have aligned in your favor and, along with plenty of hard work, you've got a hit on your hands. Or the President and Congress are focusing positively on your issues. Or a galvanized community is hot to pitch in. Or, ironically, a natural disaster or human tragedy starkly reveals the significance of your mission.

Again, to help frame the message in light of the target audience, the Task Force should—without undue modesty or stars in its eyes—list its awareness of:

- Accurate and positive perceptions of the organization, its programs, or the organization's general field of work

- Helpful media attention on the organization's issues

- Market segments actively seeking exchanges with the organization

- High demand or enthusiastic support for what the organization offers

- The organization's reputation as a leader or change agent
- Awards and formal recognition the organization has received

Now turn to the receptivity portion of Worksheet 3, Section 3C (page 155).

## 4. Develop emotional content

Effective messages strike a chord with both the head and the heart. What you need here is again right at hand: Task Force members themselves are sure to have been deeply impressed by what your organization does. To elicit emotional content, ask all Task Force members to:

- Describe something about the organization's work that has most touched or affected them and why
- Share the personal meaning they experience in the organization's mission
- State the most compelling reason why someone should support your organization

Turn to the emotional content portion of Worksheet 3, Section 3D (page 156).

## 5. Draft key messages

This step is completed by a writer, an editor, or a small group. The answers recorded on Worksheet 3, Sections 3A–3D, provide the raw material for distilling key messages into the following necessary forms:

- Case statement
- Results in achieving your mission
- Slogan, tag line, or both
- Persuasive statements

On the facing page are examples of key messages for Samaritan Bethany Foundation, the fund-raising arm of an organization that serves the aging in Southern Minnesota.

## Key Messages of Samaritan Bethany Foundation

### Case Statement

No one is immune to aging. As we live into our 70s, 80s, 90s, and—increasingly—our 100s—each of us will face the need for anything from a helping hand around the house, to nursing services in our home, to a move into a senior community or skilled-care facility. Demographic trends clearly predict a dramatic increase in the number of elderly Americans.

Samaritan Bethany is the leading provider of a full continuum of care for aging persons in Southern Minnesota. Our ongoing goal is to provide holistic health services and congenial living environments to all those in our area who need them, regardless of individual financial circumstances. To accomplish this goal now—and in the face of spiraling needs—we are asking the community to support the development and provision of these critical services. For our parents, ourselves—and eventually our children—each of us has a critical stake in the vision that all aging persons live with dignity and loving care. Please join Samaritan Bethany in realizing this vision in Olmsted County.

### Results of Our Work

- Through our home health care agency, we make it possible for people who are recovering from serious injuries or who are growing frail with age to live and be cared for in their own homes.
- We make it possible for older adults to live with family members by providing daily activity and support services at our adult day center.
- We developed an independent living facility so older adults can maintain maximum independence as long as possible.

- We make nursing home environments dignified and as pleasing as possible.
- We reduce expensive health care costs for the elderly by providing "just-what's-needed" home and community-based services.
- We continuously develop innovative approaches and make them available to all in our community.

### Slogan

Samaritan Bethany
*For aging with dignity and loving care.*

### Persuasive Statements

- It's what we want available for our parents . . . and for ourselves. *(Segment: children of aging parents.)*
- The return on your investment with Samaritan Bethany is a community that cares for its older adults. *(Segment: local business owners and corporations.)*
- It's important that *everyone* in our area ages with dignity and loving care. With government support in question and a growing elderly population, Samaritan Bethany Foundation needs your help to do even more. *(Segment: families of those served, staff, volunteers, and past donors.)*
- Your gift helps Samaritan Bethany pioneer new programs and services in our community—all to benefit the elderly. *(Segment: major donors and community leaders.)*
- Through a partnership with Samaritan Bethany, your church or community group can make its own mark on growing needs for care, service, and companionship for the aging. *(Segment: congregations and service clubs.)*

The Task Force should assign the task of developing draft messages and a deadline for its completion. Worksheet 3, Section 3E (page 157) provides a format for presenting proposed messages.

## 6. Amend and approve messages

*A mind is a terrible thing to waste.*

*Ignore your teeth and they'll go away.*

*Dick Drank. Dick Drove. Dick Died. Don't Be a Dick.*

*When you can't breathe, nothing else matters.*

*Reduce, reuse, recycle.*

*The family that prays together, stays together.*

Every so often lightning strikes and we deliver high-impact messages that do the job and more. Your key messages need to do the job for you—and for your marketing representatives—based on the list of criteria you developed. Here is a process to use as you apply the criteria:

1. Post the list of criteria so everyone can refer to it.
2. Ask Task Force members to rate draft messages from 1–5 based on the criteria. (1 = Doesn't meet criteria, 5 = Completely meets criteria)
3. Share ratings and discuss the results. If messages don't get a strong rating, specifically cite how they fall short.
4. Make suggestions for how messages could be improved.
5. If messages need to go through another draft, ask the writers or editors to consider Task Force feedback and return another set of drafts.
6. Repeat Steps 1–6 if necessary.
7. Before final approval, make sure Task Force members are genuinely pleased with your messages and would be confident using them.

Use the seven steps above to amend and approve your key messages.

### *Message testing*

No matter how good your messages seem to you, it's unwise to take your own word for it. A little external message testing can go a long way. You may choose to go about it informally, by showing your messages to family members and friends outside the organization for reactions. Or you may choose to conduct more formal tests through one or more focus groups with representatives from your A-list.

Whichever method you choose, outside reaction can either reinforce that you're on the right track or send you back to the drawing board with great new information.

Message testing can be conducted as you proceed with the next steps in this workbook. Set a deadline for test results and delegate message testing to a small subcommittee of the Task Force. Once the results are in, the Task Force should reexamine the key messages and make changes, give final approval, or, if necessary, return to earlier steps in message development and produce new drafts.

An approach to message testing is outlined in Appendix A (page 105).

## 4. Set Communications Strategy
### Select the materials and techniques you will use to convey key messages

Goals, segmented and prioritized audiences, and key messages are the superstructure for your communications strategy. At this point, expert guidance is helpful—and for large-scale efforts, it's essential. Marketing communications specialists bring a full set of options, many cost-saving techniques, and a professional hand to the development of promotional materials. Whether they are staff members, volunteers, or paid consultants, one or more specialists should lead the Task Force in assessing communications needs and developing a full set of recommendations with a clear rationale and budget estimate for each.[3]

The following are basic materials needed to directly support marketing representatives:

- A key-message reference sheet with case statement, results, slogan or tag line, and persuasive statements

- A fact sheet, brochure, or information packet

- Presentation scripts and overheads

- Appropriate letterhead and thank-you notes

- At least one gimmick to spice things up and stimulate word-of-mouth advertising (pins, refrigerator magnets, picture postcards, T-shirts, and so on)

When affordable and needed, additional audiovisual tools such as video, slide, or flexible computer-based presentations can be extremely effective.

Marketing communications specialists bring a full set of options, many cost-saving techniques, and a professional hand to the development of promotional materials.

---

[3] *A more complete process to help select communications techniques is provided in* Marketing Workbook Volume I.

These materials and techniques help back up in-person promotion efforts:

- Public relations tools such as a master news release and set of background materials
- Advertising
- Media relations
- Special events
- Public speaking
- Telemarketing
- Web page
- Marketing partnerships or sponsorships provided by other organizations

This is also the point to discuss and decide the number and type of *cultivation events* you will include in your strategy. Cultivation events are "warm-ups" to solicitations that follow the cultivation. These events range from large gatherings with crowd appeal to small, intimate get-togethers. At some point in any cultivation event, a marketing representative provides a brief formal or informal explanation of the purpose of the promotion effort and a general request to respond. Some presentations go further in outlining the specific levels of support desired. People are informed what will be coming their way in terms of solicitation and may be asked to fill out an initial response or pledge card. Examples of cultivation events are:

- A series of dinners-for-sixty hosted by the parish priest to explain the need for a larger church and rally support for the upcoming capital drive
- United Way campaign kickoffs that may revolve around community volunteerism, stadium-style boosterism, or both
- Student-led campus tours
- Privately hosted opening-night receptions
- One-on-one or small group invitations to breakfast, lunch, dinner . . . you-name-it
- Site visits
- Backyard barbecues
- Neighborhood meetings
- The ever-popular round of golf

The number and type of events to hold depend on the scope of your effort, what will appeal to your prospects, and the extent to which you believe they need to be warmed up.

Worksheet 3, Section 4 (page 159) provides a format to outline your communications strategy.

## 5. Affirm Goals and Strategies
### *Be sure the Task Force agrees the plan will work*

To complete Step 3, the Task Force steps back from its work to make sure the whole picture fits together. Here are questions to help the Task Force assess its work so far:

1. Are your goals realistic and achievable?

2. Do targeting, key message, and communications strategies clearly build on one another? Does your plan feel *doable?*

3. Are the benefits of the effort worth the costs? Are budget estimates for communications in line with available or attainable funds?

4. Does the plan give you a sense of confidence and momentum?

If strong reservations come up when discussing these questions, it's time to stop and take stock. Some plans—no matter how they look on paper—just don't feel right. Identify each person's concerns and talk them through. Some Task Force members may be on board, but not quite ready to bubble with enthusiasm until seeing actual results. Others may correctly identify potential difficulties or barriers. Make needed adjustments. If you run up against problems you can't solve, seek expert advice.

Worksheet 3, Section 5 (page 160) will help you question and affirm your goals and strategies.

DETERMINE ROLES, PEOPLE TO INVOLVE,
AND RECRUITMENT TECHNIQUES

# Determine Roles, People to Involve, and Recruitment Techniques

There are four major roles your marketing representatives may assume to help reach prospects and move them toward the exchanges you want. Some representatives will play a single role, while others will participate in two, three, or all four ways. The roles are:

- Ambassador
- Door-Opener
- Cultivator
- Solicitor

In addition, your marketing effort may need one or more people in leadership roles—a working campaign chair who sets the pace, an in-name-only honorary chairperson, or an inspirational chairperson who leads from behind by firing up the troops.

One-to-one solicitation is the ultimate results-getter—and has a worse reputation than it deserves—but it is not the only job, nor the best job, for everyone. In Step 4, you will assign a recruitment coordinator, set recruitment goals, determine which roles are needed, match them with lists of potential participants, create brief job descriptions for your marketing representatives, and make a recruitment plan.

**Who to involve in this step:**
*The Marketing Task Force and a person with human resources knowledge.*

# 1. Assign a Recruitment Coordinator

*Note: All coordinator roles throughout the effort may be held by one person or may be shared. One Task Force member should be involved; however, it helps build support for the effort to bring in others from outside the Task Force.*

The major job duties of the recruitment coordinator are:

- With Task Force input, coordinate all aspects of marketing representative recruitment
- Assemble and train a team of people to carry out recruitment efforts

The responsibilities of the recruitment coordinator include:

1. Schedule a mini-training session for recruiters, extend invitations to the training sessions, and track RSVPs
2. Organize lists of potential marketing representatives
3. Gather and finalize recruitment materials
4. Plan content and oversee the training session for recruiters
5. Follow up with recruiters
6. Track results and report them to the Marketing Task Force
7. Thank everyone involved
8. Conduct a brief evaluation of the recruitment effort

It is now time to assign a recruitment coordinator.

# 2. Decide Needed Roles and Set Recruitment Goals

With the scope, goals, and strategies of your effort already in place, you can now decide what roles are required and determine the number of marketing representatives you will recruit for each role. Here are descriptions of the four roles.[4]

- *Ambassadors:* The seed-scattering role. Can be taken on by large numbers of people. Requires willingness to represent the organization, both formally and informally, in the ambassadors' communities. Asked to be alert as "scouts," identify prospects, and pass names along for follow-up. High performers make the most of networking, often exchange business cards, and leave an informative and engaging impression whenever the subject of your organization or cause pops up.

---

[4] *A set of tips for each of the four major roles is provided in Appendix C and included in the* Pocket Guide for Marketing Representatives.

- ***Door-Openers:*** The in-the-wings role. Can be taken on by a fairly large number of people. Requires willingness to provide names of and information about prospects. Asked to allow use of their names in making contacts and, in some cases, to sign introductory letters, make phone calls, and accompany solicitors on calls to smooth the way. High performers make the most of their address books and prove the rule *it's not what you know, but who.*

- ***Cultivators:*** The warm-up role. Generally taken on by a limited number of people. Requires willingness to make personal invitations. Asked to host prospects for anything from elegant dinner parties to rounds of golf to breakfast at the local greasy spoon. High performers make the most of their social circles and are happy to expand them on your behalf.

- ***Solicitors:*** The bring-it-home role. Often accepted once fears and concerns are addressed. Requires willingness to gain commitments from individual prospects. Asked to make personal contacts, take the lead in a request, and participate in follow-up. High performers make the most of every minute with a prospect, enjoy the role, and play it somewhere between a sport and an art.

Now it is time to set goals for the number of marketing representatives you will recruit for each role. Think it through as follows:

- Ambassadors: There is no limit to the number of Ambassadors you might recruit. The more people who know your marketing goals and are on the lookout for potential prospects, the better.

- Door-Openers: The number of Door-Openers depends on the number of doors you need to open. Do you already have good access to your target audiences? Or will you need a significant number of introductions to get you inside?

- Cultivators: To decide how many cultivators you'll need, revisit your target audiences and your communications strategy for reaching them. The number and type of cultivation events planned dictate the number of people you need in this role.

- Solicitors: The number of solicitors required depends on the number of prospects to be reached one to one and how many calls you plan to assign to each solicitor. Look back at your target audiences. Approximately how many people will you solicit? How many prospects per solicitor? What about additional solicitors who may be willing to make just one or two calls?

The overriding question is, "How can we bring the greatest number of people into this effort?" You can multiply your outreach when people take on more than one marketing representative role.

Turn to Worksheet 4, Section 1, Question A (page 163) to determine the marketing representative roles needed in your effort and to set recruitment goals.

## 3. List Prospective Marketing Representatives

On Worksheet 1, Section 2, you identified groups of potential marketing representatives and approximate numbers in each. Now you will create a full list of names and decide who can best recruit whom.

In most cases, Ambassadors are listed in groups rather than as individuals. This pertains especially to staff, board, and other standing groups. You will be more in touch with Door-Openers, Cultivators, and Solicitors, so it is necessary to have individual names and contact information.

Turn to Worksheet 4, Section 1, Question B (page 164) to list prospective marketing representatives and determine whether you have sufficient prospects to meet your goals.

## 4. List Recruiters

A recruiter's role is to contact prospective marketing representatives and recruit them to participate in your effort. In smaller campaigns, Task Force members may do all the recruiting. In larger efforts, organizational leaders and others are often tapped for help with recruitment. Whether the campaign is large or small, put yourself in the place of your future marketing representatives as you decide who can most effectively help them say *yes!* to your request.

Turn to Worksheet 4, Section 1, Question C (page 166) to list people who will recruit prospective marketing representatives.

Once you have compiled names of prospective marketing representatives and recruiters, complete Worksheet 4, Section 1, Question D (page 166). Assign each prospect to a particular recruiter. Then create individual lists for each recruiter with names and contact information for the individuals or groups he or she should contact.

At this point you will need to consider an important choice that may be a matter of organizational policy. While participation in promotion campaigns is usually optional for volunteers, some boards of directors require it of their members. Marketing representative roles may also be included in formal job descriptions of paid staff. A clear decision should be made regarding the extent to which participation in promotion efforts is mandatory.

## 5. Develop Mini-Job Descriptions

A job description for each role will help you recruit marketing representatives. A simple format (provided on Worksheet 4, Section 2, page 167) can be followed or amended as the Task Force thinks best. The format calls for you to explain:

- Goals of the effort
- Marketing representative role description
- Responsibilities
- Approximate number of contacts to be made (for Cultivators and Solicitors)
- Requested length of service
- Number of meetings and training sessions to attend

Mini-job descriptions are an important recruiting tool. Volunteers and staff want to know just what they are being asked to do and find it reassuring that duties are clearly spelled out. But don't forget that while being a marketing representative is work, all your communications about it should be positive and upbeat. In the example that follows, a United Way has some fun spoofing typical job descriptions at its training session for recruiters.

---

### ★ *Make $40 million in less than 7 months!* ★

WANTED: Extremely busy people for long hours. Requires asking friends, associates, and complete strangers for money and convincing them to do same with others. Enthusiastic team building and coaching with large workforce of borrowed people. Must enjoy troubleshooting, have a *"uniting way"* about you ☺, and say "thank you" continuously. Armed forces recruitment background a plus. If engaged, must attend early morning training sessions, call in every week, and expect to be asked for gifts.

---

Creating mini-job descriptions is best done by a subgroup of the Task Force. If there is any difficulty making them short and to the point, ask someone with human resources expertise for help.

Turn to Worksheet 4, Section 2, (page 167) for the job description format.

## 6. Determine Recruitment of Campaign Chairs

The final discussion item for your recruitment plan is whether there will be a chair or cochairs for your campaign, who might fit the role, and who will recruit them. The Task Force should now make these decisions.

DEVELOP A MASTER TIMELINE AND
ACTION PLAN FOR THE EFFORT

# Develop a Master Timeline and Action Plan for the Effort

In the final step to Ready the Organization, you create a master calendar for rolling out the promotion campaign and assign responsibilities and deadlines to ensure everything falls into place. In this nuts-and-bolts step, you outline plans and select coordinators in six areas:

1. Production of communications materials
2. Motivational training
3. Follow-up and support
4. Reward and recognition of your marketing representatives
5. Celebration of success
6. Evaluation of the effort

Although there are six distinct coordinator roles, in smaller campaigns they might all be taken on by one or two people. In larger efforts, coordinator roles are likely to be more widely distributed. Think through possible candidates for all coordinator roles before making assignments and remember, coordination can be a shared job.

### Who to involve in this step:

*The Task Force, a marketing communications specialist, a training specialist, a reward and recognition specialist, and those who will provide coordination and support during the marketing effort.*

# 1. Develop an Overall Calendar and Schedule for Production

In Step 3, you identified elements of your communications strategy. Now you will lay out the overall calendar of the promotion effort and set a schedule for production. There's a bit of "back and forth" in this process as you look at optimal dates, consider the amount of time necessary to prepare, and assign coordinators.

Turn to Worksheet 5, Section 1, Question A (page 169) and think ahead to the overall effort. You need to decide:

1. When recruiters will be on board and trained

2. When recruiters will contact potential marketing representatives and engage their participation

3. Target dates for motivational training sessions for marketing representatives

4. An official kick-off date

5. Dates for any special events

6. Other events already on the calendar you might coordinate with, such as an annual meeting, graduation, or performance

7. Deadlines for particular phases of the effort to begin and end, such as advance solicitation, cultivation presentations and events, direct mail, full-scale solicitation, and telemarketing

8. Formal check-in dates or meetings for marketing representatives

9. An ending date for the marketing effort

10. A celebration date

11. A deadline to complete evaluation

12. Budget estimates for all of the above

Now that you have outlined the overall calendar, refer to Worksheet 3, Section 4, where you noted communications tools and techniques (page 159). Then continue on Worksheet 5, Section 1, Question B (page 170) to assign coordination responsibility and to schedule production. As you do so, you will need to answer the following questions:

1. What combination of materials, techniques, and events are we definitely going to use?

2. Who will review and approve final drafts and arrangements?

3. What are the budgets for these materials and events?

4. Based on the overall calendar, when is the deadline for each tool or technique to be ready?

5. Who can approve budget changes, if necessary?

6. Who will coordinate planning and production for tools, techniques, and events?

The process outlined above isn't actually as simple as 1-2-3. Drop-dead copy and printing deadlines coexist with a parallel world of changing schedules and last-minute *Oh-my-God-I-forgot!* requests. As deadlines approach, communications coordinators will have to continuously cross-check needs and deadlines with other coordinators. It's a two-way street, of course. Starting in Steps 6–10, these folks will be sporting lengthy checklists of their own.

## 2. Make Preliminary Plans for Motivational Training

To begin planning your motivational training sessions, you need to outline the training effort and assign a motivational training coordinator.

### Outline the training effort

Motivational training is the official beginning of the marketing effort. *All* marketing representatives should attend a two and one-half hour Ambassador training session. Door-Openers and Cultivators stay on forty-five minutes longer. Solicitors are asked to commit to an additional five-hour session.

At this point, you need to determine the types and number of sessions you will need, set tentative dates, times, and locations, and identify organizational leaders who can be on hand to extend a welcome to marketing representatives. It may be helpful to look ahead and skim Step 7 while outlining the training effort.

Many groups find it valuable to bring in outside motivational trainers or presenters to help conduct motivational training—marketing consultants, successful veterans of similar nonprofit campaigns, local leaders or celebrities, individuals who can give testimonials from personal experience. Consider seeking volunteers or hiring professional assistance if warranted.

To outline motivational training, turn to Worksheet 5, Section 2, Questions A–C (page 171).

### Assign a motivational training coordinator

The motivational training coordinator is the point person for the range of activity associated with planning and holding training sessions. This individual (or team) is responsible for implementing the plans outlined by the Task Force.

The responsibilities of the motivational training coordinator include:

1. Finalize schedule of training sessions, issue invitations, and track RSVPs

2. Organize prospect lists

3. Gather and finalize materials

4. Plan session agendas

5. Handle logistics

6. Get training information to marketing representatives unable to attend sessions

7. Thank participants and wrap up the training sessions

8. Gather evaluation feedback

Return to Worksheet 5, Section 2, Question D (page 171) to assign a motivational training coordinator.

## 3. Think Through Follow-up and Support

Once your marketing effort is launched—no matter how inspired—it will only be kept afloat with continuous, systematic follow-up and support for the marketing representatives.

- On-the-ball Ambassadors and Door-Openers will be calling in and faxing information on hot prospects. *Routing is needed.*

- Participants in motivational sessions will leave ready and willing to take on their new duties, only to run into stiff competition from already demanding to-do lists. *Reminder calls are needed.*

- There will be crises-of-confidence, questions, and unforeseen situations. *Reassuring support is needed.*

- Cultivators and Solicitors will be in nearly constant contact as dates are set, invitations are sent, and calendars are synchronized. *RSVPs and arrangements are needed.*

- And you will have success! *Reports and acknowledgments are needed.*

Specific follow-up and support tasks include:

1. Maintain a master list of all marketing representatives, their prospects, and their progress.

2. Route new prospects.

3. Make reminder calls.

4. Provide reassurance, respond to questions, and ensure follow-up on opportunities, problems, and special needs.

5. Handle RSVPs.

6. Handle arrangements for meetings and events.

7. Issue immediate acknowledgments and thank-yous to prospects who say yes and to others who participate or contribute in some way while the promotion campaign is in progress.

8. Tabulate results and issue interim and final reports.

9. Be a liaison to the communications coordinator to ensure periodic "broadcast" reminders and communication of success stories, progress toward goals, and thank-yous.

10. Provide administrative support.

Successful follow-up and support require clear accountabilities and continuous coordination. Turn to Worksheet 5, Section 3 (page 172) to assign a coordinator and to determine who will handle individual follow-up and support responsibilities.

> It's easy to neglect the meaning of mission-based work—to forget those moments that "give nonprofit goose bumps."

## 4. Plan Rewards and Recognition

Every marketing representative you recruit shares at least one motivation: they care about your organization, its mission, and what you bring to the world. Their best reward is a share in your success. Throughout the campaign, anyone and everyone who contributes in the least way should be acknowledged, thanked for each thing they do, and continuously reinforced for the importance of their participation. When the promotion campaign draws to a close, it will be time to give formal recognition to all who participated.

### Determine rewards

It's easy to discount or neglect the meaning of mission-based work—to forget those moments that, in the words of one executive director, "give nonprofit goose bumps." We reward our marketing representatives when we remind them they are protecting children, or making art part of everyone's life, or giving the gift of education, or saving the sea. Consider the approach of the nonprofit leader in the following example:

### Mission: The Prime Motivator

Out-going-after-twenty-seven-years executive director of Children's Home Society of Minnesota, Roger Toogood (yes, there are endless puns) never fails to thank all those working on behalf of Children's Home for what they do *for children*. It isn't for Roger or for the organization. It's for children. Toogood, who is renowned as an advocate, guided the course of one of the most effective nonprofits in the country and is a natural marketer. Under Toogood's leadership, Children's Home Society developed comprehensive marketing plans including people-based promotion efforts that have led to sustained growth, even during tough years of government cutbacks and increased competition. Children's Home was recognized for its success with an award from the Child Welfare League of America. Toogood extends the credit to every marketing representative—whether a board member calling on a major funder, a staffer driving 350 miles to meet potential adoptive parents, or a senior volunteer arriving for her phone shift—by kindly reminding them of what they are doing *for children*.

Everyone planning the marketing effort and providing leadership, follow-up, and support can reward marketing representatives with reminders like Roger Toogood's: *You have made the world a better place. Thank you.*

Then it's time to go for lunch. After all, there's more to life than meaningful work. Motivation comes in diverse packages and any number of small perks are due your marketing representatives. A bouquet of thank-you balloons, a beautiful card, or lunch at a favorite spot does a great deal for the morale of the troops.

Worksheet 5, Section 4, Questions A and B (pages 173–174) will help you brainstorm rewards for marketing representatives, choose the best ideas, and set a rewards budget.

### Plan recognition

Authors Russ Prince and Karen File present a superb research-based segmentation of major donors in their book *The Seven Faces of Philanthropy*.[5] They also highlight four categories of contribution for which donors appreciate recognition—and point out that few nonprofits consistently provide recognition for all four ways of contributing. People want to be recognized:

- **Fund-raising efforts**
  Raising funds may or may not be the focus of your promotion effort. If you have another type of goal—recruiting volunteers or selling season tickets—then recognition is in order for the work done and the numbers brought in.

---

[5] *Copyright 1994, Jossey-Bass Publishers, San Francisco.*

- **Volunteer activity**

  Many of your marketing representatives will contribute to the promotion campaign by participating on task forces or committees, helping with special events and mailings, and pitching in on a variety of other odd jobs. These volunteer activities (or staff performances above and beyond duty) are all deserving of recognition.

- **Recruiting other volunteers**

  Okay Task Force members, this one's for you—and those who help you recruit marketing representatives and other volunteers. Mobilizing people is a significant achievement and should be recognized.

- **Personal contributions**

  In many cases, board members, staff, and current volunteers are among nonprofits' most generous contributors. If you are planning a fund-raising campaign, your marketing representatives are top-rated prospects who will merit recognition for their gifts. If you have a different focus for your effort, it is still likely that both in-kind and monetary contributions will be made. Recognition is in order.

There are classics in formal recognition—handsome wall plaques always stay in style, as do newsletter, annual report, and wall-of-honor listings. But the best recognition is more personal—whether it be renaming the rotunda of the museum for the fifty-year trustee or presenting a gift-wrapped bottle of spicy sauce to your "hottest" Solicitor. As with the high school yearbook tradition of humorous and serious predictions, you can recognize every marketing representative as "most likely to succeed," "most congenial," or "most likely to forget appointment calendar." Recognition items can range from the crystal vase to the whoopee cushion.

Turn now to Worksheet 5, Section 4, Question C (page 175) to list the best ideas for recognizing your marketing representatives and set a recognition budget. As you do so, bear in mind the four categories in which contributors value recognition.

## Assign a rewards and recognition coordinator

The responsibilities of the rewards and recognition coordinator include:

1. Ensure everyone involved with the promotion campaign is frequently reminded of the value and importance of their work

2. Oversee the presentation of tangible group and individual rewards

3. Decide how to provide individualized recognition

4. Oversee selection, ordering, and receipt of recognition items

5. Plan and orchestrate formal recognition

Turn to Worksheet 5, Section 4, Question D (page 175) to assign a rewards, recognition, and reenlistment coordinator. (While only rewards and recognition have been discussed in this section, reenlistment also falls in this coordinator's job. Reenlistment is discussed in Step 9.)

## 5. Assign Celebration and Evaluation Coordinators

It is hard to think about the end of your campaign when it hasn't even begun. All you need to decide at this point is who will be in charge of celebration and evaluation. Responsibilities are detailed in Step 10.

Turn to Worksheet 5, Section 5 (page 175) to assign these coordinators.

*The more people who know your purpose and hear your message, the better.*

# Readiness Wrap-Up

Congratulations! The marketing effort is mapped out and you're nearly ready to go. There are four steps to wrap up Ready the Organization.

### 1. Get final endorsements

While leaders of the organization have been connected to the process all along, it is still advisable to gain formal endorsement from the executive director, top management, the executive committee or full board of directors, and possibly other staff or volunteer groups. Expect some helpful suggestions for improvement in your plans. Accepting new input, even at this point, builds broader ownership for the effort.

### 2. Allocate or raise necessary funds

When the total budget for your effort is added up, you may need more money than you originally thought. Promotion is based on an investment-return philosophy, so don't short yourself at the front end. If projected results are worth it, a reach into cash reserves or a round of special funding requests may be in order.

### 3. Communicate organization-wide

As soon as you are ready to begin recruitment, let *everyone* know about the promotion effort. As you set out on the path to achieving your goals, the more people who know your purpose and hear your message, the better. Some may be impressed and ask to join the effort. By all means, welcome them and find a spot to work them in!

## 4. Decide how to manage your effort

If you will be orchestrating a promotion effort solo, you'll have your hands full—but at least it will be easy scheduling meetings of the team! Most efforts do have multiple coordinators, so a system of overall management has to be decided. You may go for a central coordinator at the top, a self-managed coordination team, or any number of other management variations. Decide what will work for you . . . and schedule your first meeting.

That's it! Take a pause to refresh, because it's time to put the show on the road.

*Marketing in a non-profit organization becomes effective when the organization is very clear about what it wants to accomplish, has motivated everyone in the organization to agree to that goal and to see the worthwhileness of that goal, and when the organization has taken the steps to implement this vision.*[6]

— Philip Kotler

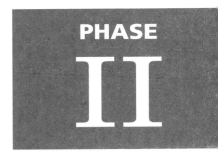

# *Mobilize Your Marketing Representatives*

During Phase I, you set a solid foundation for carrying out your promotion campaign. In Phase II, you'll build on that foundation to achieve marketing results and prepare your organization to continue mobilizing people for ongoing marketing success. There are five steps in Phase II:

---

[6] *From* Managing the Non-Profit Organization *by Peter F. Drucker, copyright 1990, HarperCollins, New York City.*

IMPLEMENT THE RECRUITMENT PLAN

# Implement the Recruitment Plan

Your efforts up to this point have been about getting ready—and there's more planning to come—but now you shift gears and go public. The plans you developed to this point list *whos, whats, wheres,* and *whens,* plus outlines of *how.* In Step 6 you begin the nitty-gritty of implementation. Coordinators swing into action, details are attended to, tools and techniques materialize, recruiters get trained, and you post your first results. You conclude this first step in mobilizing your marketing representatives with a brief evaluation and an opportunity to mark success.

**Who to involve in this step:**

*Recruiters, logistical support, internal presenters, and an outside trainer if desired. Recruitment coordinators take the lead.*

Following is the set of planning and action steps to implement the recruitment phase of your marketing effort. Worksheet 6, Section 1 (page 177) provides a recruitment coordinator checklist.

## 1. Schedule a Mini-Training Session

Take a quick look at the work ahead in this step, and then schedule a two-hour mini-training session with your recruiters, giving as much advance notice as possible. You'll also be confirming presenters for the session, possibly including an outside trainer. Recruiters who haven't been involved to this point will need an invitation that includes a brief description of the overall effort and the role you want them to take. Otherwise all you need for now is a date, time, place—and enough time to get ready. The agenda and materials come later.

## 2. Organize Recruitment Lists

Refer to Worksheet 4, Section 1, and develop prospect lists for each recruiter. Include names and contact information for potential marketing representatives the recruiter is to approach. When you create these lists, make spaces for recruiters to note each marketing representative's:

- Agreement to participate
- Availability for motivational training date(s)
- Any special communication or follow-up needed

## 3. Gather and Finalize Materials

You have already created many materials and lists to be used by the marketing representatives. In advance of the training session, distribute:

- Written summary of the background, purpose, and goals of your marketing effort
- Key messages (case statement, results of your work, slogan or tag line, persuasive statements)
- Mini-job descriptions
- Individual recruitment lists

Needed for the training session:

- Recruitment letter that states the purpose and goals of your promotion effort, the role you are asking an individual or a group to take on, a brief summary of the job description, and either a direct request to RSVP or an explanation of what the next step will be. In some cases, form letters are fine, while others may require a more personal approach.
- Phone or presentation scripts that provide guidance, key points, and often exact wording for recruiters who will be making direct contact with your prospective marketing representatives.
- Presentation overheads (see the training guide on pages 69–71).

## 4. Plan the Recruiter Training Session

It's desirable that all recruiters attend the training session, but make exceptions as you think best. Make sure you can provide training information to those who do not attend. A sample agenda for a two-hour session is provided below; a guide for training follows. Feel free to make changes as you plan your own agenda.

## Sample training agenda

---

**Organization Name**
*Slogan or tag line for your marketing effort*

**Marketing Representative Recruitment Training**
Date, time, place

### Goals

1. Develop understanding of the overall promotion effort and the role of recruiters.

2. Clarify roles of prospective marketing representatives and the amount of time they are being asked to commit.

3. Build recruitment skills.

4. Build enthusiasm for the recruitment effort.

| Agenda | Minutes |
|---|---|
| A. Welcome, introductions, goals for the session | 10 |
| B. Overview of the promotion effort and recruitment plan | 5 |
| C. Questions and discussion | 5 |
| D. Recruitment methods | 20 |
| E. Review of letters and scripts | 5 |
| F. Marketing representative job descriptions | 20 |
| G. How to address questions, concerns, and requests when recruiting | 20 |
| H. Practice session | 20 |
| I. Timeline for recruitment | 5 |
| J. General questions and discussion | 5 |
| K. Adjourn | 5 |

Total time: 2 hours

---

## Training guide

### A. Welcome, introductions, goals for the session          *10 minutes*

In some promotion campaigns, this meeting simply pulls together a half-dozen Task Force members; in large campaigns, this meeting convenes a large cast of new players. Give an appropriate welcome, make introductions, and review goals for the session.

### B. Overview of the promotion effort and recruitment plan          *5 minutes*

Ask recruiters to review the background materials you sent them. Use overhead transparencies to go over key points and the timeline.

*5 minutes*

## C. Questions and discussion

People may have many questions as you go along. Keep this brief discussion focused on the big picture.

*20 minutes*

## D. Recruitment methods

People who aren't familiar with recruiting need some help figuring out how to go about it. Here is a list of ways to reach potential marketing representatives:

- **Potential chairpersons** need one-to-one attention.

- **Staff groups** are easy to reach through announcements, presentations, memos, posters, and E-mail.

- **Managers and supervisors** should be informed through memos and in meetings to ensure their understanding and support.

- **Boards, advisory committees, and volunteer groups** can be reached by letter, at regular meetings and gatherings, and by phone and E-mail.

- **Those beyond your inner circle** generally require presentations or personal invitations.

- **All of the above** can be reached through informal conversation, newsletter announcements, news releases, and whatever additional means you choose.

Make an overhead transparency with the methods you recommend for your recruiters and give a few minutes for recruiters to note how they will approach their prospective marketing representatives. Respond to questions, and be open to suggestions. If recruiters have specific questions about people on their list, handle them outside the meeting.

*5 minutes*

## E. Review of letters and scripts

Hand out letters and phone or presentation scripts and give people a few moments to review them.

*20 minutes*

## F. Marketing representative job descriptions

Ask recruiters to review the marketing representative job descriptions in small groups and talk through how they would present them (in the most positive light!) to potential participants. Reconvene the large group and discuss each small group's suggestions. Explain that recruiters need to be receptive to the input and requests of each potential marketing representative they contact. This may include helping potential marketing representatives redefine their own roles or signing them up for a role different from the one they were originally asked to fulfill.

### G. How to address questions, concerns, and requests when recruiting

*20 minutes*

Give the large group five minutes in pairs to come up with the questions, concerns, and requests they believe they'll hear from potential marketing representatives. Quickly list them, and then work with the large group to come up with responses. Record these responses and distribute an edited question-and-answer sheet after the session.

### H. Practice session

*20 minutes*

Have each member of the group find a partner. Give them ten minutes each to role-play a recruiting attempt. Encourage them to coach one another along. Remind them their goal is to get a *yes*. Take a moment at the end of this practice session for the group to share insights gained from practice.

### I. Timeline for recruitment

*5 minutes*

Remind people of deadlines. Tell them how to report the results of their recruiting efforts to the recruitment coordinator.

### J. General questions and discussion

*5 minutes*

Be sure to let people know whom they can call with questions or challenges that arise as they begin recruiting marketing representatives.

### K. Adjourn

*5 minutes*

Conclude the session with big thank-yous to all recruiters, a few motivational comments, and a warm good-bye!

Adapt the training agenda in any way you think best. Think through which members of the Marketing Task Force should take the lead on each agenda item and make sure they are prepared. You may feel you have plenty of internal expertise to conduct the training or you may find a motivational trainer with recruitment expertise to facilitate parts of the agenda. Once everything is set, it's time to distribute advance materials, finalize details, and conduct the training.

## 5. Follow Up with Recruiters

The question-and-answer sheet promised during training should be prepared and distributed immediately after the session. In addition, individual follow-up may be needed on questions, concerns, and suggestions raised in the training. This is also the time to provide training information to any recruiters who could not attend.

Midway through your recruitment period, call recruiters to see how they're doing and to make sure they're on track. As soon as you reach your deadline, follow up immediately with anyone who has not turned in his or her results.

## 6. Tabulate Results and Thank Recruiters

Once results are in, recruitment coordinators should tabulate them and develop final lists of marketing representatives including their names, contact information, role(s), and any important comments or notes about their participation. These lists should be forwarded to those coordinating motivational training, follow-up and support, and reward and recognition.

Recruiters deserve a hearty thank-you for their work. Be sure to call and send notes!

## 7. Finalize Prospect Lists

In Step 7, you will need to provide Solicitors with lists of the prospects they are to contact. Recruitment coordinators should convene Marketing Task Force members for an "assignment meeting" to prepare these prospect lists.

To develop prospect lists, work from Worksheet 3, Section 2B, where you segmented and prioritized your target audience. At this point, you will need the individual names and contact information for groups and individuals you consider to be prospects. A prospect list format is provided on Worksheet 6, Section 2 (page 180). A sample is provided on the facing page.

## 8. Evaluate the Recruitment Effort

The results of your recruitment plan are a bellwether for the overall effort. Convene the Task Force for a brief evaluation session to determine how you did and what you learned. Use Worksheet 6, Section 3 (page 182) to respond to these questions:

1. Did we achieve our recruitment goals?
2. If not, what did we misjudge or fail to foresee?
3. Did the recruitment process go smoothly?
4. What have we learned that will help us as we go on?
5. Do we need to revise any part of our plans?
6. If we judge our recruitment effort a success, how should we celebrate it?

To conclude Step 6, make any needed revisions to your plans and mark your success.

Marketing Representative: <u>Lorraine Knight</u>

### Middlebury Women's League
*Join a second century in progress.*

**Our goal:** One hundred new members per year in 1999, 2000, and 2001, bringing us from 1,000 to 1,300, a 30% increase over 3 years.

**Our effort:** First annual one-month fall membership drive.

**Our target audience:** All Middlebury women twenty-five years old and older.

**Priority segments:**

- Lapsed members
- Daughters of members
- Members' friends, relatives, and work associates
- Community leaders

- Women with young children
- Women new to the community
- Single women
- Women just leaving the workforce
- Women in nontraditional relationships

**Prospect List:**

| Prospect | Deadline to contact | Deadline to report in |
|---|---|---|
| **Organizations/groups to contact for presentations:** | | |
| 1. Middlebury Women's Professional Network | 9/15 | 11/15 |
| Dr. Angela Roth-Martin | | |
| 2626 Parklands S. #422 | | |
| Middlebury, State 54321 | | |
| Work: P: 555-4321 F: 555-4320 E-mail: none | | |
| Home: N/A | | |
| Notes: *Angela is member and would like presentation at a regular Network meeting* | | |
| 2. Women's Inter-Faith Council | 9/15 | 11/15 |
| (Name, address, etc.) | | |
| **Individuals for personal contact:** | | |
| 1. Beth Cleveland | 10/1 | 11/1 |
| (address, phone, etc.) | | |
| Notes: *Grandmother was a founder, youngest just left for college* | | |
| 2. Marva Frye | 10/1 | 11/1 |
| (address, phone, etc.) | | |
| Notes: *Was active, lapsed in 1995, former president of African-American Heritage Society* | | |
| 3. Janet Anderson-Alexander | 10/1 | 11/1 |
| (address, phone, etc.) | | |
| Notes: *New in town. Elaine Alexander is mother-in-law* | | |
| 4. City Council Member Maria Alvarez | 10/1 | 11/1 |
| (address, phone, etc.) | | |
| Notes: *Reportedly interested—many women in her ward are members* | | |
| 5. Crystal d'Canter | 10/1 | 11/1 |
| (address, phone, etc.) | | |
| Notes: *Received Young Leadership Award for work with AIDS hospice, known to support our issues; well-connected with singles* | | |
| 6. Stacy Kotsopulos | 10/1 | 11/1 |
| (address, phone, etc.) | | |
| Notes: *Been busy with twins who are just entering school* | | |

HOLD MOTIVATIONAL TRAINING

**Step 7**

# Hold Motivational Training

When you get to Step 7, everything starts happening at once. In large-scale campaigns, communications teams cluster around newly arrived materials (to assorted cheers and groans) while special event teams look like they're training for the Olympics. Energy also rises in more modest efforts, and no wonder: whether it's a group of fifteen or a cast of thousands, you're about to assemble the people who will make your vision a reality.

The focus in Step 7 is planning and conducting motivational meetings. In this step you will confirm participation in training, set agendas, gather and finalize materials, handle logistics, and actually launch your marketing effort. Step 7 also introduces the *Pocket Guide for Marketing Representatives* as a tool you can provide marketing representatives.

**Who to involve in this step:**

*Marketing representatives, administrative support, executive director or board chair, promotion effort chairpersons, and outside trainers if needed. Motivational training coordinators take the lead.*

Worksheet 7 (page 183) provides a to-do checklist for planning and conducting motivational training.

# 1. Finalize Schedule of Training Sessions

The number and types of motivational training sessions you conduct are based on the scope of your effort, the number of marketing representatives involved, whether they are staff, standing volunteer groups, or new recruits, and the number and types of roles people have agreed to take on. Guidelines for scheduling sessions are:

1. Pulling all marketing representatives together at once is most desirable, but may be impractical. *Advantage: builds the most energy and excitement.*

2. Coordinating training with standing meetings, such as staff, board, and advisory committees, greatly eases scheduling challenges. *Advantage: can be very efficient.*

3. Mixing staff and volunteer groups is healthy. *Advantage: everyone learns from hearing new perspectives.*

4. Ambassador training is the foundation for all roles and is provided in a two and one-half hour session. For other roles:

   • Door-Openers and Cultivators have a forty-five-minute add-on session following Ambassador training.

   • Solicitors have an additional in-depth five-hour session.

   Schedule solicitation training as a separate follow-up session. *Advantage: trying to pack it all into one day is just too much.*

5. Motivational training should serve as a kickoff to the promotion effort; after training, marketing representatives should be encouraged to begin their work immediately. *Advantage: you've got momentum out of the gate.*

Using these guidelines, look ahead to sample agendas and logistics that follow, and then turn back to Worksheet 5, Section 2 (page 171) to revise and finalize the schedule for motivational training.

The following case study shows the dramatic impact motivational training can have—even on seasoned nonprofit leaders.

**When Opportunity Knocks—Training Pays!**

The director of a day care center in a suburban county is a participant in Ambassador and Door-Opener training as part of a broad promotion effort of the center's large parent organization. She has long considered promoting the day care center part of her responsibilities, but has had little exposure to training—and has never been part of an organization-wide effort.

As she later tells it, "Something clicked in the Ambassador training. After that I was more aware of opportunities. I started putting together what people were looking for with the benefits we, as a total agency, could provide them."

When she hears that a large local hospital is shopping for a community-based partner for its well-attended annual costume ball fund-raiser, her new-found marketing antennae perk up. Honing in, she learns that the hospital wants a nonprofit with a household name (her parent agency is a century old), a good reputation (parents love her center and the parent agency is well-respected statewide), and a communications staff to augment the hospital's own public relations efforts (her center regularly wins communications awards).

She phones into headquarters for guidance on writing a proposal and takes the lead in making a presentation. The end result is an agreement that nets the day care center $150,000 per year for three years—their share of proceeds from the annual ball.

## 2. Gather and Finalize Materials

Following are lists of the material to be prepared for motivational training sessions.

For distribution *in advance* of training sessions:

- Written summary of the background, purpose, goals, major elements, and timeline of your marketing effort
- Key messages: case statement, results, slogan or tag line, persuasive statements
- Individual prospect lists (for Solicitors)
- Sample communications piece for your effort, such as a brochure or fact sheet
- Cover letter reiterating date, time, and place of training, plus dates and times of any future meetings or group activities

For distribution *during* training sessions:

- Agenda
- Phone or presentation scripts and materials
- Master prospect list
- Unassigned prospect list
- Communications materials to be used by marketing representatives
- *Pocket Guide for Marketing Representatives*
- Follow-up and report forms (A blank form for Door-Openers and Cultivators can be found in Appendix B, page 116.)

## 3.  Plan Training Sessions

Successful training sessions produce three valuable outcomes: (1) you broaden knowledge of your marketing goals and so immediately increase the likelihood of their being met; (2) marketing representatives gain skills and instruction necessary for their particular roles; and (3) your overall effort builds momentum.

The outline for training sessions is:

- All marketing representatives: 2 ½ hours (Ambassador training)
- Door-Openers and Cultivators: 3 ¼ hours (one 45-minute segment added on to Ambassador training)
- Solicitors: 8 ¼ hours (Ambassador training, plus Door-Opener/ Cultivator session, plus separate five-hour session for Solicitors only)

A set of sample agendas for motivational training sessions follows on pages 79–81. Each sample agenda begins with goals for that particular session followed by a timed outline. Fully annotated training guides can be found in Appendix B. No worksheet is provided for developing session agendas. In drafting your training sessions, feel free to follow the formats provided or to modify them in any way you think best. Consider internal as well as external presenters. Think through who should take the lead on each item and make sure they are prepared.

## Ambassador training sample agenda

*Introduces all marketing representatives to the promotion effort; provides tools, techniques, and practice to enable Ambassadors to scout potential prospects; kicks off your campaign.*

---

### Organization Name
*Slogan or tag line for your marketing effort*

### Marketing Representative Training for Ambassadors
Date, time, place

**Goals**

1. Broaden knowledge of the goals, audience, and key messages for the promotion effort.

2. Clarify the Ambassador role and develop skills for carrying it out.

3. Ensure participants' understanding of how to obtain follow-up and support.

4. Have a good time and build enthusiasm for the effort!

| Agenda | Minutes |
|---|---|
| A. Get settled, welcome, introductions, goals for the session | 10 |
| B. What it's all about | 10 |
| C. Overview of the marketing effort | 15 |
| D. Mission and results | 20 |
| E. Target audience | 10 |
| F. Break | 10 |
| G. Breaking the ice, determining interests, identifying a prospect | 15 |
| H. Key messages, conveying customer feedback | 45 |
| I. Wrap-up | 15 |
| J. Social time | Varies |

Total time: 2 hours, 30 minutes

## Door-Opener/Cultivator training sample agenda

*Teaches specifics of carrying out Door-Opener and Cultivator roles; secures participants' commitment to particular actions; provides opportunity to distribute follow-up forms for participants to fill out. Door-Openers and Cultivators hit the ground running!*

### Organization Name
*Slogan or tag line for your marketing effort*

**Marketing Representative Training for Door-Openers and Cultivators**
Date, time, place

### Goals

1. Clarify roles of Door-Openers and Cultivators and explain how to carry them out.
2. Complete follow-up forms.
3. Review timeline and tasks.
4. Respond to questions and concerns.

### Agenda                                                                      Minutes

A. Goals for the session ............................................................... 5

B. Door-Opener and Cultivator roles ...................................... 10

C. Tips ............................................................................................ 5

D. Work on follow-up forms ...................................................... 15

E. Next steps and deadlines, response to questions .................. 5

F. Adjourn ..................................................................................... 5

Total time:  45 minutes

## Solicitor training sample agenda

*Builds skills and confidence for both novice and veteran Solicitors; addresses fears and concerns; confirms scheduling of solicitations; puts in play the most powerful promotion technique—one-to-one contact!*

**Organization Name**
*Slogan or tag line for your marketing effort*

**Marketing Representative Training for Solicitors**
Date, time, place

### Goals

1. Develop comfort and confidence with the solicitation process.

2. Set personal marketing goals and build skills to achieve them.

3. Ensure participants' understanding of deadlines and how to access follow-up and support.

4. Have a good time and build enthusiasm for the marketing effort!

| Agenda | Minutes |
|---|---|
| A. Get settled, welcome, introductions, brief review, goals for the session | 15 |
| B. Great solicitations | 10 |
| C. Know your prospects | 10 |
| D. The good, the bad, and the ugly | 30 |
| E. Break | 10 |
| F. The Solicitor Five-Step (overview) | 10 |
| • The warm-up | 10 |
| • Introduce the subject | 20 |
| • Interview for needs, introduce benefits | 30 |
| • Make the request | 30 |
| • Close | 15 |
| G. Break | 15 |
| H. Solicitation role play | 40 |
| I. Fears, concerns, questions | 20 |
| J. Confidence builders and personal marketing goals | 15 |
| K. Review of assignments, timeline, and system of follow-up and support | 10 |
| L. Adjourn | 10 |

Total time:  5 hours

## 4. Handle Logistics

Whether add-ons to regular meetings or stand-alone events, everything about these sessions should speak *motivation.* That means food, fun, and festivity. Training coordinators should be sure to provide the following amenities:

- A convenient location, accessibility, parking
- Good seating, a room just the right size, a flip chart, and audiovisual equipment
- Refreshments or meals
- Decorations, posters, displays
- Background music for gathering, social, and break times
- Staffed welcome-table
- Materials organized for easy distribution
- Name tags
- Other fun or festive touches

Once these logistics are set, it's time to distribute advance materials, finalize details, and conduct the sessions.

## 5. Provide Training Information to Marketing Representatives Unable to Attend Sessions

It's critical that all marketing representatives attend a training session. Make sure you are prepared to provide one-to-one or small group make-up training for anyone who can't attend. Written summaries of motivational training usually fail to pack enough punch without personal instruction.

## 6. Thank Participants and Wrap Up the Training

A thank-you-for-coming note to marketing representatives makes for easy and immediate reinforcement. Coordinators, presenters, administrative support staff, and others who helped plan and conduct motivational training deserve special pats on the back.

During training your marketing representatives may have expressed needs for particular kinds of follow-up and support. In addition, you may have made changes or additions to individual prospect lists. Make sure to get such information to follow-up and support coordinators immediately.

## 7. Gather Evaluation Feedback

Motivational sessions should drive to an up-beat finish. Don't stop for an extensive evaluation process, but do get some feedback. Gather comments for your overall evaluation at the conclusion of your effort. Make immediate follow-up contacts with a representative sample of those who participated in the training—people you can trust to give you honest impressions. Write up a summary of the feedback you receive and put it aside for reference in Step 10.

• • •

With motivational sessions completed, you should be flying high! But don't get blown off course . . . with your marketing effort now off the ground, you'll need both feet firmly planted as you implement your system of follow-up and support.

PROVIDE ONGOING FOLLOW-UP AND SUPPORT

# Step 8

# Provide Ongoing Follow-up and Support

No matter how motivated, mature, or masterful they appear, your marketing representatives are most likely to succeed when they have a well-organized, attentive, and responsive stage crew behind them. One-to-one promotion is the high-visibility part of marketing. Follow-up and support happens behind the scenes and makes a world of difference for those out under the bright lights. In Step 8 you will attend to the *Five Rs* of Follow-up and Support: Routing, Reminders, Reassurance, RSVPs, and Reports. You will also ensure that all prospects who say yes receive prompt acknowledgment.

In Step 8 you will attend to the *Five Rs* of Follow-up and Support: Routing, Reminders, Reassurance, RSVPs, and Reports.

The training you provide Solicitors should include a brief discussion of how to convey customer feedback. One-to-one promotion efforts are an ideal opportunity to learn how your prospects view the organization and what you might do to improve the quality of your products and service. Instruct Solicitors to greet such feedback openly—just as you should. Pass the feedback—negative and positive—to people in the organization who can respond to it.

### Who to involve in this step:

*Marketing representatives, administrative support staff, those in the organization with knowledge and experience to provide guidance and help solve problems. Follow-up and support coordinators take the lead.*

Follow-up and support is a job of many fine details. Worksheet 8 (page 187) provides a checklist that follow-up and support coordinators can use to stay on top of the work.

## 1. Orient the Follow-up and Support Team

A range of talents and skills, plus just plain lots of time, is required for effective follow-up and support. Rarely will one person cover all of this alone. Your first job is to pull the team together and set up systems and individual responsibilities. You might also line up a few "troubleshooters" in the wings—the executive director or board chair—who are brought in only for unique opportunities or problems.

## 2. Update the Master List

At this point, you need a continuously updated master list of prospects. This list notes who is assigned to follow up with each marketing representative, and it should provide a means to track representatives' progress. This master account list should also be used for tracking additions, new assignments, and reassignments.

## 3. Route New Prospect Names to Marketing Representatives

During motivational training, you asked Door-Openers, Cultivators, and Solicitors to complete and return prospect identification, assignment, and activity forms (found on page 116). Some of these forms were handed in during training, and others were promised later; some marketing representatives asked to be contacted for their information. Follow-up calls with those who requested them should occur as soon as possible. Calls on promised items should take place the day following your agreed-on target date. If questions on prospect lists or other topics came up, be timely in addressing these issues as well.

As soon as you have names and contact information on new prospects, route them to specific marketing representatives for door-opening, cultivation, or solicitation. Routing of new prospects is likely to continue throughout your marketing effort and sometimes beyond its official end. Follow-up on leads must be thorough and immediate and, at times, must include confirmation back to your source that what he or she suggested was done. When possible, combine routing information with routine reminder calls.

## 4. Send Reminders as Needed

A target date for returning forms is only one of many deadlines you may have set with marketing representatives. Follow-up coordinators should track all such deadlines to ensure marketing representatives receive necessary reminders.

In some cases you're simply calling to check *in:*

> *Is everything going all right? How are you doing on your appointments? If there's anything you need, please make sure to be in touch. Thanks for everything. I'll check in again week after next.*

At other times, it's two days past deadline and you're calling to check *up:*

> *It's just a little past report-in time. How are things going? Can you get it in today? Is there anything we can do to help? Thanks for doing so much.*

Regrettably, there are also calls to someone who seems to have checked *out:*

> *Hi, me again. How's it coming? We really need to get things cleaned up. Could we go over what's left? We've got people who ended up with a little extra time on their hands. What if we shift these prospects to them? Great! How about if I take your report right over the phone. Thanks!*

It's wishful thinking to imagine a world where no one needs reminders. We're all busy and a friendly comrade urging us along is generally welcome. Handled in the right spirit, reminders are a nice boost to those who receive them. Besides, the squeaky wheel gets the grease.

Coordinators should stay on top of reminders and get support to any marketing representative who needs it.

## 5. Reassure Representatives as Needed

Anybody can use a little reassurance from time to time—especially Cultivators and Solicitors. Here are a few of the situations you're likely to run into . . . suddenly, you're marketing's answer to Ann Landers.

### *Dear Crisis in Confidence:*

> *It's absolutely normal to have cold feet—especially if this is your first time out. Best if you can talk out whatever is troubling you. Perhaps all you need is a refresher on the basics, a little shoring up, or a few exact pointers on what to do next. If you're the learn-by-doing type, go ahead and plunge in, you'll be fine. If you like everything planned down to the "t," then let's review details— I'll bet you've got it covered. Remember the big picture—the mission. And remember,* **you can do it.**

### *Dear Let's Go over It One More Time:*

> *Let's say I'm you're prospect. We'll walk through it. You contacted me, so you start. Whoa, slow down. Try a few pleasantries to break the ice. Remember to gauge my pace; then gently take charge.*

*Go ahead and introduce the subject at hand. Just an appetizer portion. Good. Ask me a direct question. And one or two follow-ups. Okay, time to reinforce what you heard, speak to my concerns, and pop the question. Perfect. Let's confirm a closing. Great! Now, we can get a partner out with you once or twice if you'd like . . . .*

### Dear Stuck with Old Baggage:

*Every so often this is bound to happen. Customer research shows people who feel wronged usually tell their story ten times. Some wounds stay open even longer. First thing is to hear it out. Next say you're sorry it happened. Then see if you can move along on a better note. Ask if there's anything you can look into and try relating some of your own positive experience. If nothing helps, perhaps things are best left where they are. If your prospect appears willing to set the baggage aside, try for a fresh start.*

### Dear Feeling Put Off:

*Don't take it personally. There's an old marketing maxim that says you make the sale on the tenth contact with your tenth prospect. Every contact counts—letters, calls to schedule (and reschedule) appointments, thank-you notes for meetings, a business moment at a social gathering. Add them up and ten isn't all that much. As for the tenth prospect, good advance screening sometimes reduces the odds. Most important, keep after folks. There are prospects out there who will respect you for not giving up. Unless somebody clearly tells you to lay off, they're still a live one.*

### Dear Hooked a Big One:

*So she wants six presentations to separate work groups by Wednesday—three on the night shift. That's fantastic! Good that you E-mailed for help right away. As for that couple who are reluctant to contribute this year because they heard it's better to get started on an endowment, let them know we're eager to talk again. We'll team you up with a specialist. And excellent news on the senior center that wants a group discount on tickets. We hadn't thought about doing it that way, but it makes sense, so let's. The church youth advisor wants to send* how *many volunteers? Say, what's your secret?*

### Dear Nothing Seems to Be Going Right:

*More than a bad day, huh? Could be astrological, but let's go over what you're doing and see if we can spot anything wrong. It may just be that persistence thing. Not that we want to badger anyone, but it can take a lot just to get through. You* are *getting through? If they don't want to see you, did you try just going ahead on the phone? You did. They all said no and you're halfway down your list. Let's run through a sample conversation . . . sounds like you're doing fine; you must've gotten all the toughest nuts in town. Could be you need some new prospects who are better bets. You deserve to get a yes.*

***Dear Square Peg:***

*Good for you for giving it a try! You're right; some people just aren't cut out for this. No sense driving yourself to a nervous break-down, so let's just chalk it up to experience. Once the pressure's off, I'll bet you'll enjoy being a low-profile Ambassador. In the meantime, maybe you'd like to work on the celebration. Goodness knows you'll be happy when it's over!*

Your marketing representatives were given names of people to contact should they have questions or need support. Any time you touch base with marketing representatives, you may also hear reports of customer feed-back and advice. Be available and follow up as soon as possible. If questions or situations come up that stump you, make sure to find someone with the appropriate expertise to help strategize a response. Remember, "I'm not sure, I'll get back to you" is a wiser choice than off-the-cuff advice.

## 6. Send RSVPs

This form of follow-up must be tight and precise. In large campaigns, the volume of scheduling, rescheduling, and confirming can be enormous. As you support your marketing representatives, you may be juggling their needs with those of individual prospects, presenters, tour guides, and various VIPs, not to mention caterers, balloon sculptors, and the occasional string quartet. Invitations, appointments, and arrangements are by now a way of life.

Allow nothing to chance. Better to confirm and *re*confirm every rendez-vous than leave anyone high and dry.

## 7. Compile Results and Communicate Progress

Compiling results as you go helps you track and communicate progress, alerts you if your effort needs shoring up, and provides a check-in point to verify prompt acknowledgment to *yes* prospects.

Reporting at regular intervals boosts morale when things are good and lets everyone know extra effort is needed if they're not. In some cases—such as building campaigns with construction contracts pending—early returns are watched intently. In general, there's no cause for alarm if your effort gets off to a slow start. Some races are won out of the gate; others at the finish line.

Coordinators need to ensure that accurate numbers are being used, that everyone responsible for generating reports is on task, that the right people are receiving reports, and that acknowledgments and thank-yous are quick and complete.

Follow-up, support, and communications continue throughout the life of your promotion effort—anywhere from a few weeks to several years to, as illustrated in the following case example, a sophisticated and permanent system.

---

### Building a 6,000-Volunteer Pyramid—Each Year

Every summer, when the sun broils the pavement of New York's inner city neighborhoods, The Fresh Air Fund sends thousands of children on a free vacation in the country, an experience few of them otherwise would have. They are the guests of over 6,000 eastern seaboard host families in a thirteen-state, one-province "Friendly Town" network running from Ontario to Virginia.

In an upside down pyramid structure, a small paid staff provides direct follow-up and support to 50 volunteer regional "Fund Representatives" and 325 "Friendly Town Chairpersons." In turn, these volunteers recruit local teams to carry out public relations activities, identify, contact, and screen prospects, and sign on families willing to open their homes to Fresh Air kids who may never have walked barefoot in the grass.

"Most people hear about hosting a Fresh Air kid for some years before they do it," explains executive director Jenny Morgenthau. Door-opening, cultivation, and solicitation efforts ("We depend on volunteers to sell the program to their friends . . . ") are supported by a steady stream of communications strategies and high-visibility collaborations with the likes of fashion designer Tommy Hilfiger, pop star Mariah Carey, and the *New York Times*. The toll-free number never stops ringing. New prospects are routed continuously.

Host family recruitment materials, how-to manuals, and videos on screening techniques are regularly updated to be as user-friendly as possible. "The world has changed," states Morgenthau. "People have less time. We provide many more mechanical things, like computerized lists, mailing labels, and public relations materials customized for local use." Every January, the 50 Fresh Air Fund representatives are brought to Manhattan for motivational training and every second year the 325 Friendly Town chairpersons join them. What goes on? "We thank them *a lot*," Morgenthau emphasizes, "and help them learn the necessary skills to do their jobs back home. We bring in national speakers and former Fresh Air kids . . . things that make the volunteers feel good and show them how grateful we all are."

Indeed, Morgenthau quickly hands the lion's share of credit to the hard-working people who commit themselves as volunteers. But they aren't out there alone. Few nonprofit marketing efforts are better researched or refined. The Fresh Air Fund stands as a model of leveraging resources for cost-effective and compelling results.

Follow-up and support is ongoing throughout the life of your promotion effort. Implementation of this step may be weeks, months, or even years in length. If you are conducting a longer campaign, be sure to build in rewards and interim celebrations as morale-boosters along the way.

REWARD, RECOGNIZE, REENLIST

# Reward, Recognize, Reenlist

In the early 1960s, my father's sales force ran an incentive program. If everybody made their quotas on Kahlua, all the guys and their wives got a week in Acapulco. Every two weeks during the campaign my mother received another tiny sombrero, colorful Mexican straw horse, or similarly symbolic trinket with notes encouraging her to imagine the sunlight on the sea and keep being the woman behind her man. They all came back with gorgeous tans. (Not to suggest anything nearly so retro, but hey, it worked.)

In Step 5, you brainstormed a more updated (and probably less pricey) list of rewards. Now it's time to give them out. It's also time to finalize recognition plans and implement a modest reenlistment effort.

**Who to involve in this step:**

*For reward and recognition: everyone. For reenlistment: chairpersons, coordinators, and nominating groups. Reward and recognition coordinators take the lead.*

A checklist for reward, recognition, and reenlistment coordinators is provided on Worksheet 9 (page 189).

## 1. Provide Tangible and Intangible Rewards

Everyone associated with the marketing effort can:

- Say thank you and remind people of the importance of what they're doing
- Ensure behind-the-scenes workers are included
- Bring treats to meetings and gatherings
- Send notes and *You're a star!* stickers (or whatever communications gimmick you've chosen)
- Come up with spur-of-the-moment ideas of their own

Reward and recognition coordinators should:

- Implement plans for group rewards such as lunches, special time off, midpoint parties, and flowers
- Make sure everyone who needs help with arrangements or rewards materials gets the help they need
- Come up with—and pass along—new ideas

The best reward is success. Make sure to touch base with your communications coordinator to broadcast kudos for both individual and collective performance.

## 2. Implement a Formal Recognition Plan

In Step 5, you set up a formal recognition plan. Coordinators may already be awaiting the delivery of plaques, certificates, wall-of-honor bricks, paperweights, monogrammed director's chairs, and other such public and private tributes.

Respect those who wish their contributions played down and go as far as possible with those who want publicity for what they've done.

Recognition coordinators also need to be gathering information throughout the promotion effort to prepare for personalized recognition. Chairpersons, other coordinators, and those providing follow-up and support can help uncover the best angle for each marketing representative or, at a minimum, a group of all-stars. Look for the serious and the humorous. Respect those who wish their contributions played down and go as far as possible with those who want publicity for what they've done. Don't forget your original Marketing Task Force, the chairs of the campaign, volunteers who may have come and gone, vendors, and others whose talents were a help along the way.

Your upcoming celebration is the ideal place for formal recognition, although some presentations are best offered in less public settings. Only in rare circumstances should recognition take place long distance. If people can't attend an event, try to find some way to reach them in person.

## 3. Reenlist

Some annual promotion efforts begin the same day they end. If you're on a year-round cycle—or even if you're not—you may already be thinking of the future. In some organizations, being named chair or a key coordinator is seen as quite a plum—another form of recognition. Announcing such appointments as the promotion effort ends makes a nice burst of energy for the next campaign. There may also be marketing representatives you'd love to keep involved in other ways. This can be an excellent opportunity to explore future possibilities.

Current chairs, coordinators, nominating groups, and others looking ahead should consult together, determine reenlistment possibilities, and assign people to meet with and gain agreement from future leaders.

The promotion effort is winding down now—or heating up for a final push. In either case, you're in the home stretch. Good cause for celebration!

CELEBRATE SUCCESS AND EVALUATE THE EFFORT

# Celebrate Success and Evaluate the Effort

Success doesn't mean you achieved every goal you set. Granted, we'd all like to unveil over-the-top results, but—outcomes aside for a moment—the fact that you conceived, planned, and carried out a promotion campaign is a success in itself. You've tried new approaches, stretched your skills, found efficiencies, faced difficult circumstances, learned lessons, put in countless hours, and given every part of it the best you've got. All of these things are worthy of celebration.

There is a worst-case scenario: an effort that falls so short of its goals it's hard to deem it anything but a failure. Unless someone ran off with the proceeds, try to avoid laying blame and save post-play analysis for just a bit. In the meantime, there's a celebration to be had—even if it's more like a wake.

As soon as things quiet down, you will close out your effort with an evaluation.

**Who to involve in this step:**

*Celebration: everyone. Evaluation: executive director, board chair, or both, Marketing Task Force members, chairpersons, coordinators, others who helped plan or support the effort. Party planners and evaluation coordinators take the lead.*

A checklist for celebration coordinators is provided in Worksheet 10, Section 1 (page 191). An evaluation outline follows in Worksheet 10, Section 2 (page 192).

> The fact that you conceived, planned, and carried out a promotion campaign is a success in itself.

# 1. Celebrate!

So now comes, for many, the single best job—planning the party. Celebrations of success run the gamut: grab a formal dinner gown; loosen your tie after work; pack plenty of bug spray for a potluck in the park. This event needs to be geared to the tastes of your marketing representatives. Not that you're likely to turn down donated all-day family passes to the amusement park. And not that you'll please everybody or that some shouldn't broaden their horizons. Still, unless your crew is terribly adventurous, abide by the guideline of providing the most fun for the most people within the range your budget will allow.

Regardless of venue, *everybody* who contributed to your marketing effort should be invited and organizational leaders must be there.

## Determine celebration concept

This is the fun part. Following is a list of questions to help you plan your party. These are also incorporated in the checklist on Worksheet 10, Section 1 (page 191).

- What type of party will it be?
- When will it happen?
- In what great spot?
- What food will be served?
- Are alcoholic beverages appropriate? If so, what arrangements will be made for responsible use?
- How about recorded music, live entertainment, amateur skits, or other wild ideas?
- What formal recognition will occur? (Keep speeches short.)
- What else will make it festive and fun?

## Handle logistics

This should be old hat by now! Details range from designing invitations to ordering food to checking off RSVPs to decorating name tags. These and many other details are included in the checklist for celebration coordinators.

## Have a great time!

What more need be said? You deserve it.

## 2. Evaluate the Promotion Effort

Marketing evaluation is a straightforward undertaking. There are three major evaluation questions you need to answer: (1) Did we achieve our goals? (2) Did we implement our effort effectively? (3) What do we need to research or refine for the future?

Good evaluation tells us what to keep doing and where to rethink or improve. We analyze the past to benefit the future: we're looking for keys to greater success. Some organizations have a long-term framework and analyze both year-to-year results and long-term trends. Other campaigns are pilot projects or only carried out on special occasions, requiring project-specific evaluation. Adapt the evaluation process to produce knowledge that is valuable to your organization.

Use Worksheet 10, Section 2 (page 192) to evaluate your promotion campaign. The worksheet is formatted as a series of evaluation questionnaires. As you fill in this worksheet, pull facts and figures from final reports compiled by the various coordinators. Other evaluation questions are best answered through surveys, interviews, or focus groups, or by informally gathering opinions and impressions. To cover the discussion portions of the evaluation, hold one or more meetings with Task Force members and others who planned or carried out the effort.

> We analyze the past to benefit the future: we're looking for keys to greater success.

### Did we achieve our goals?

On Worksheets 3 and 4 you set overall goals for the effort and for recruiting marketing representatives. You have tracked results all along. On Worksheet 10, Section 2, Question A (page 192) evaluation coordinators can record both original goals and the final tallies of what you achieved.

In evaluation sessions, compare your results with your goals. Determine what contributed to a poor showing or led to success. There may have been factors beyond your control (one San Francisco group was subject to an earthquake, the Oakland fire, and the Persian Gulf War), a run of abundance (the First Lady drops in for a front-page visit), or a disaster that brings out the best in community caring. There may have been factors within your control, which are examined in the next evaluation step.

### Did we implement our effort effectively?

Coordinators are in a good position to review what happened and whether it went as planned. Following plans to the letter is not necessarily a virtue, since flexibility and creative response are often critical to success. On the flip side are poorly thought-out departures from the plan . . . or just not following through.

Each coordinator should contribute a brief summary that addresses:

1. Whether plans were followed and, if not, what was changed

2. What went well

3. Where they or others they worked with ran into problems

4. Recommendations for the future

The insights of your marketing representatives are especially important. In addition to the reports of coordinators, gather feedback and recommendations directly from marketing representatives. Ask about problems, successes, and the quality of training, materials, and follow-up and support.

Coordinators should respond to evaluation questions using Worksheet 10, Section 2, Question B (page 193). Record the perspectives of your marketing representatives on Worksheet 10, Section 2, Question C (page 194).

## What do we need to research or refine for the future?

As you answer questions about the outcomes and implementation of your promotion campaign, you'll generate new questions about areas that need further research or refinement.

### Research

Some questions get answered with more questions. That's when research is called for. The most frequent evaluative findings that lead to research are:

1. *Surprise successes*: When something produces much better results than anticipated, it's important to know why. Success may have been a fluke, or a sign of a hidden vein in the market ready to be mined.

2. *Surprise failures*: Same as above in reverse. You can soften the blow of failure by learning from it. Failure can signal the need for new strategies, expose flaws in systems and planning, or tell you a particular segment is tapped out.

3. *Possible trends*: Marketers who conduct cyclical promotions monitor and compare various factors to identify potential trends. Such customer information can lead to product changes such as shorter, more episodic volunteer jobs. Or the trends may indicate a need to shift the emphasis between making new friends and keeping the old. Similarly, one or more market segments may perform differently than expected, suggesting you need more information to tell you why.

4. *Possible improvements*: When it *is* broken, then you need to know how to fix it. Research may mean surveying best practices, delving more deeply into the needs of marketing representatives, getting expert comment on communications materials, shopping for improved information systems, and so on.

## Refinements

Some conclusions will pop right out: "Motivational training on a Saturday turned out great. Let's schedule that way again." "People didn't wear their buttons. We need something they'll actually *use* next year." "*Everybody's* got to make their calls. We need to follow up better and have reserve callers." "Prospects who went on building tours were most likely to say yes. Let's remember that." "Big givers wanted detailed results and financials. Our reports have to be expanded and our Solicitors need to be trained on this."

Some refinements are more elusive and may generate strong differences of opinion. It's important to set aside pride of ownership, pay attention to facts, observations, and feedback, and discuss the issues openly. Take lessons from what went wrong, take a respectful look at tradition in light of today's world, and don't be afraid to abandon tired strategies in favor of innovation.

Worksheet 10, Section 2, Question D (page 195) provides space to list research questions and recommended refinements in each of the ten areas of the promotion effort.

## Did we learn and change?

On Worksheet 1 you described how your organization's capabilities or skills might be enhanced by the promotion effort. Take time in your evaluation session to reflect on these facets of your overall purpose. There are two questions:

1. What did we learn?
2. How did our organization change for the better?

Worksheet 10, Section 2, Question E (page 197) provides space to summarize answers to these questions.

## What are our next steps?

Evaluation should lead to action. How can you follow up on what you have found? On Worksheet 10, Section 2, Question F (page 198), you conclude the evaluation by defining how evaluation findings will be passed on to inform future efforts.

# Postscript

In early 1995, a small vocationally oriented regional college was in crisis. A projected cut in state aid meant possible pink slips for a number of faculty members unless enrollment could be increased by four hundred students the coming fall—a virtually unheard of prospect. The chair of the Business and Economics Department came up with the idea of putting faculty out on the high school recruitment circuit as marketing representatives, a radical plan. By the end of spring semester, fall enrollment was up by 675 students. In a *New York Times*[7] story on the unusual endeavor, an instructor said, "We have to recognize that the health of the college as a whole depends on the individual activities of every one of us."

The stakes were high, the response swift, and the results extremely good news, not just for those with jobs on the line, but for the *students*. Many of them might have missed out on college without the unusual, personalized approach that included help completing financial aid applications and professors' home phone numbers for questions and coaching once they got to school. Everyone went the extra mile—and everyone benefited from the results.

> Nonprofits cannot afford to hold back. Not for our own survival, but for what we are here to accomplish.

Every mission-based organization has a similar opportunity—and obligation—to pull out all the stops. *The stakes are always high.* Government has narrowed its scope, the business of business will always be profit, and society is in the midst of extraordinary and painful transformation. Some say the most extraordinary in history. Some say the future viability of the planet hangs in the balance. Nonprofits cannot afford to hold back. Not for our own survival, but for what we are here to accomplish.

Three final points:

1. Don't buy the big lie about shrinking resources. They're *shifting,* not shrinking.

2. If Margaret Mead was right, and a small group of thoughtful, committed citizens can change the world, just think what a dedicated corps of nonprofit marketing representatives can do.

3. The health of the whole depends on the individual activities of every one of us.

Plan and promote! Ask for the exchange! You've got it in you—as does everyone who cares for your cause.

There is everything to gain.

---

[7] *"A college links raises for teachers to recruiting of students" by Joseph Berger,* New York Times, *June 10, 1995.*

# Message Testing

The power of message testing is borne out in the example of a Jewish federation that piloted its key messages with a small group of leading donors. "Not farsighted enough," the organization was told. "We know what good you're doing in the community. We want to hear that you're making an impact at the state capital and collaborating with others committed to strong social support systems." The federation took its customers' input seriously, made plans to beef up government relations, and quickly revised key messages to reflect this new emphasis. It went on to a most successful campaign.

## 1. Conduct Interviews or Focus Groups with Key Sources of Support

Except in very complex campaigns with multiple A-list target audiences, message testing can be done with a small sample group. Simply come up with ten to twelve individuals who each represent a key source of support—either because of their personal capacity or their desirability. You'll probably be able to reach two thirds of the people you identify. If that number seems slight and you'd like more input, increase the pool of potential invitees.

You may do one-to-one interviews or conduct focus groups. Interviews can be scheduled at mutually agreeable times and places. For focus groups:

1. Pick a pleasant, convenient location and see to logistics.

2. Choose an experienced facilitator, preferably one who is not a staff member or highly visible volunteer. Go over the sample agenda with the facilitator and ask what would make it comfortable and effective in his or her view.

3. One or two Marketing Task Force members may be present to listen at focus groups, although their presence can inhibit participants' responses. On the other hand, it is extremely valuable to hear and see participants' reactions firsthand. Use your best judgment on this.

4. If you like, make preparations to audiotape your sessions. Be sure to get consent from participants to be recorded when you invite them.

5. Confirm acceptance to participate by letter, and call with a reminder the day before the focus group.

## 2. Follow a Prepared Format for Interviews or Focus Groups

The following format and questions can be used for both interviews and focus groups. Feel free to modify the phrasing, especially in the more informal setting of one-to-one conversations. In focus groups, questions 1–4 should be answered by each person in turn. Questions 5 and 6 can be open for group discussion.

1. Open any interview or focus group session with a round of introductions to help people feel comfortable.

2. Ask, "On a scale of one to five, with five being *very familiar*, please say how familiar you are with [name of organization or cause] and a little bit of what you know about it."

3. Hand out the key messages for your campaign—the case statement, the statements showing the results of the work your organization does, the slogan or tag line, and the persuasive statements. Give participants time to read them. Then ask, "Overall, on a scale of one to five, with five being *very positive* and one being *very negative*, what is your response to what you have just read?"

4. After each participant has answered question 3 in turn, find out the reason for each person's response. You might say, "Now please tell me a little about your response . . . why you gave the rating you did."

5. Next, explain how you intend to use the statements: "These messages may be used to help encourage people to [state type of exchanges you want]. Please say if you believe they will be effective and why or why not." Encourage a group discussion. Then proceed naturally into question 6 below.

6. "What suggestions do you have for improvement or for different or additional messages?"

7. When the discussion seems to be winding down (or time is running out), thank each person for participating in the focus group (or interview).

## 3.  Summarize Results and Act on Them

1. Prepare a summary of message-testing results.

2. Use the results with the Marketing Task Force to confirm your messages as effective or to pose possible suggestions for improvement.

3. Information from message testing may require action from others in the organization. If so, be sure to encourage it.

# Motivational Training Guides

This appendix provides detailed motivational training guides for:

- The Ambassador session (two and one-half hours)
- The Door-Opener/Cultivator add-on session (forty-five minutes directly after the Ambassador training)
- The stand-alone Solicitor session (five hours)

This information augments the sample training agendas provided in Step 7—which are also guides for agendas you might prepare and hand out to participants in training sessions. The annotated agendas presented here are more detailed and meant for session leaders.

This appendix also includes the Door-Opener/Cultivator Follow-up Form.

## Ambassador Training Sample Agenda

**Organization Name**
*Slogan or tag line for your marketing effort*

**Marketing Representative Training for Ambassadors**
Date, time, place

### Goals

1. Broaden knowledge of the goals, audience, and key messages for the promotion effort.

2. Clarify the Ambassador role and develop skills for carrying it out.

3. Ensure participants' understanding of how to obtain follow-up and support.

4. Have a good time and build enthusiasm for the marketing effort!

| Agenda | Minutes |
|---|---|
| A. Get settled, welcome, introductions, goals for the session | 10 |
| B. What it's all about | 10 |
| C. Overview of the marketing effort | 15 |
| D. Mission and results | 20 |
| E. Target audience | 10 |
| F. Break | 10 |
| G. Breaking the ice, determining interests, identifying a prospect | 15 |
| H. Key messages, conveying customer feedback | 45 |
| I. Wrap-up | 15 |
| J. Social time | Varies |

Total time:  2 hours, 30 minutes

## Ambassador Training Guide

*10 minutes*

### A. Get settled, welcome, introductions, goals for the session

Open the session with a welcome from the executive director, board chair, campaign chairpersons, or some combination of the three. Introduce others in key roles and, depending on the size of the group, make introductions all around. Review session goals (listed in the agenda for this session).

*10 minutes*

### B. What it's all about

This is the place for a motivational presentation. Choose one or more techniques that bring home the impact your nonprofit makes on the community. Consider an in-person testimonial from someone who has benefited directly from your services, an inspiring mini-keynote from an organizational or community leader, an audiovisual presentation, a performance excerpt, or any other attention-getting approach.

## C. Overview of the marketing effort

Ask participants to take out and review the background summary you sent them. (Have some extras on hand for those who forget.) Use overhead transparencies to summarize the purpose, elements, and timeline of the effort. Fully explain the role of Ambassadors and conclude by outlining the overall goals for the effort.

If you have not already distributed the *Pocket Guide for Marketing Representatives*, do so now. Direct participants to fill in their names and the name of the organization (after the Table of Contents of the Pocket Guide), and goals of the promotion effort (page 12).

*10 minutes for overview; 5 minutes to fill in Pocket Guide*

## D. Mission and results

Use overheads to present your organization's mission and the results it achieves.

Direct participants to pages 12–14 of the Pocket Guide to write in mission and results. Then give the group members about five minutes to continue writing how the mission and results are meaningful to them. Give them the remaining time—five to ten minutes—to share their responses with a partner or in a small group.

*5 minutes for presentation; 15 minutes for Pocket Guide exercise*

## E. Target audience

Using overheads, present the overall target audience for the effort, the A-list, and the B-list. Briefly explain how you chose these segments. Ask participants to write in the overall target audience, the A-list, and the B-list on page 15 of the Pocket Guide.

*5 minutes for presentation; 5 minutes for Pocket Guide exercise*

## F. Break

*10 minutes*

## G. Breaking the ice, determining interests, identifying a prospect

*15 minutes*

Ask group members to identify situations or settings in which they might have the opportunity to act as Ambassadors. List their responses on a flip chart.

Present an overhead titled "The Ambassador Three-Step," which lists the three phases of the Ambassador's contact with a prospect: (1) breaking the ice; (2) determining and building interest; and (3) identifying a prospect. Ask group members to think of occasions when they have already acted as an Ambassador or times when they have been engaged by Ambassadors of other nonprofit organizations, social causes, or businesses.

Next, facilitate a discussion on the following questions:

- How did these people successfully introduce their subject?
- How did they draw others out and build on their interests?
- How did these people determine you were a potential prospect and get enough information to follow up?
- In general, what makes a situation like this go well?

Continue the discussion by asking:

- When have you been put off in a situation like this?
- What have others done that was clumsy, overly pushy, offensive, or ineffective?

*Note: You can move things along by dividing your group in half and assigning each half one of the two sets of questions above. If you take this approach, conclude with a brief report from each group.*

*45 minutes as follows: 5 minutes for overview; 20 minutes for role play; 15 minutes for Pocket Guide exercise; 5 minutes for large group response*

## H. Key messages, conveying customer feedback

Using an overhead, present your key messages as things Ambassadors can say to help build interest in the organization. Then ask for volunteers for two short role-play exercises. (You may want to have volunteers planted in the audience who have agreed beforehand to do role plays if others are especially shy.) Remind your volunteers of "The Ambassador Three-Step" and ask them to include all three steps in a role-play conversation that is to last only three minutes. For the first round, ask your volunteers to do everything "wrong." In the second, ask your volunteers to do everything "right." Spend a few moments for the large group to name what was "wrong" and "right" in each role play.

Next, ask participants to work with a partner and respond to open-ended statements 6–10 on pages 16–18 of the Pocket Guide. These statements follow:

- What I will say about the organization or cause to catch people's attention
- What I will ask other people to explore their interests
- How I will bridge other people's interests to this organization or cause
- What I will do to make sure I'm in control of a next step with a potential prospect
- Being a part of this promotion effort is important to me because

Conclude this portion of the training by asking a few participants to share responses to the preceding items with the large group.

Take a moment at the end of this section to remind Ambassadors that prospects may also have messages for *them*. If Ambassadors hear suggestions or complaints about the organization or are presented with new opportunities, make sure they know who to call to report this important information.

### I. Wrap-up

*15 minutes*

Take five minutes for something fun, upbeat, and motivating: hand out your promotional gimmick, tell a story or joke you know your crowd will enjoy, bring someone out in costume to distribute candy kisses and hugs . . . be imaginative and make them smile! Then wrap up the training by leaving the Ambassadors with a few instructions as follows:

- Tell participants who to call with questions and leads on new prospects. Ask them to write these names in the Pocket Guide on page 18.
- Distribute promotional materials (brochures, organizational business cards, and so forth).
- Answer questions.
- Encourage Ambassadors to use the Pocket Guide. Suggest they read it through, carry it with them, refer to it, and use it to make notes for follow-up. Point out the tips and reminders on pages 28–31 of the Pocket Guide.

Remind Door-Openers and Cultivators that there will be an extra forty-five-minute session for them following Ambassador training, and invite everyone to spend a few minutes getting to know each other after the session ends. Close the training session with a BIG thank-you to those who planned the session and to all participants. Send them off with a rousing *Let's Go!*

### J. Social time

Leave an appropriate amount of time at the end of the session for socializing, treats, and informal question and answer.

### Total Ambassador training time: 2 hours, 30 minutes

# Door-Opener/Cultivator Training Sample Agenda

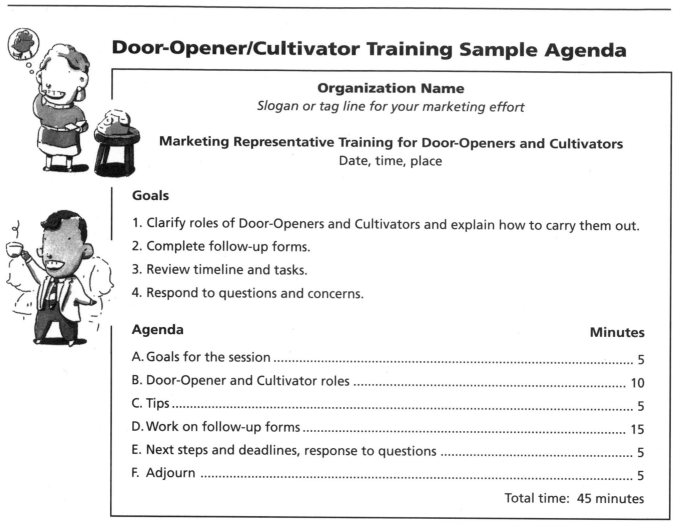

**Organization Name**
*Slogan or tag line for your marketing effort*

**Marketing Representative Training for Door-Openers and Cultivators**
Date, time, place

### Goals

1. Clarify roles of Door-Openers and Cultivators and explain how to carry them out.
2. Complete follow-up forms.
3. Review timeline and tasks.
4. Respond to questions and concerns.

### Agenda                                                                  Minutes

A. Goals for the session ............................................................... 5
B. Door-Opener and Cultivator roles ....................................... 10
C. Tips ............................................................................................ 5
D. Work on follow-up forms ................................................... 15
E. Next steps and deadlines, response to questions ................ 5
F. Adjourn ...................................................................................... 5

Total time: 45 minutes

## Door-Opener/Cultivator Training Guide

Door-Opener/Cultivator training should follow directly after Ambassador training, which Door-Openers and Cultivators should also attend.

*5 minutes*   **A. Goals for the session**

Briefly review goals for this session (listed in the agenda).

*10 minutes*   **B. Door-Opener and Cultivator roles**

Ask participants to turn to pages 7–8 in the Pocket Guide so they can follow along as you give an expanded explanation of the roles and specific responsibilities of Door-Openers and Cultivators.

## C. Tips                                                              *5 minutes*

Tips for Door-Openers and Cultivators are listed on pages 32–33 of the Pocket Guide. These are:

| **For Door-Openers** | **For Cultivators** |
| --- | --- |
| 1. Be judicious | 1. Show 'em a good time |
| 2. Give a strong personal endorsement | 2. Mix and match |
| 3. Be visible | 3. Expect to be popular |

Give participants a few moments to review the tips for their roles, and then answer any questions they might have.

## D. Work on follow-up forms                                         *15 minutes*

Distribute unassigned prospect lists (these were developed by the recruitment coordinators and Marketing Task Force in Step 6, Part 7, Finalize Prospect Lists). Also distribute Door-Opener/Cultivator follow-up forms, a copy of which appears on the next page. Talk through the follow-up form and provide any needed coaching as participants fill out their forms.

## E. Next steps and deadlines, response to questions                  *5 minutes*

Make sure Door-Openers and Cultivators understand how to contact you with feedback and that they need to get to work right away. Emphasize deadlines for returning lists. Respond to questions from the large group.

## F. Adjourn                                                          *5 minutes*

Give the Door-Openers and Cultivators a rousing farewell. It's time to get to work!

## Total Door-Opener/Cultivator training time: 45 minutes

## Door-Opener/Cultivator Follow-up Form

Name:_____

### Door-Openers and Cultivators:

1. Are there unassigned prospects you could reach to smooth the way?
   - ☐ Yes. Please check them, put your name on the list, and return it.

2. What people in your personal or professional life would you be willing to introduce to our organization?
   - ☐ I will forward a list and how I can help.
   - ☐ I would like someone to call me on this.

3. Are there people you *don't* know personally, but feel should be considered prospects?
   - ☐ I will forward a list including ideas on how to reach them.
   - ☐ I would like someone to call me on this.

### For Door-Openers only:

In what ways are you willing to open doors?
- ☐ Sign letters or invitations
- ☐ Make phone calls
- ☐ Make personal introductions
- ☐ Accompany Solicitors on visits to prospects
- ☐ Other:

### For Cultivators only:

What cultivation activities are you willing to participate in?
- ☐ Make phone calls
- ☐ Accompany Solicitors on visits to prospects
- ☐ Attend a cultivation function
- ☐ Make presentations
- ☐ Host a party or an event
- ☐ Host a few individuals
  Types of activity: (for example, breakfast or lunch at a restaurant, a round of golf)

- ☐ Additional cultivation ideas:

## Solicitor Training Sample Agenda

**Organization Name**
*Slogan or tag line for your marketing effort*

**Marketing Representative Training for Solicitors**
Date, time, place

**Goals**

1. Develop comfort and confidence with the solicitation process.

2. Set personal marketing goals and build skills to achieve them.

3. Ensure participants' understanding of deadlines and how to access follow-up and support.

4. Have a good time and build enthusiasm for the marketing effort!

| Agenda | Minutes |
|---|---|
| A. Get settled, welcome, introductions, brief review, goals for the session | 15 |
| B. Great solicitations | 10 |
| C. Know your prospects | 10 |
| D. The good, the bad, and the ugly | 30 |
| E. Break | 10 |
| F. The Solicitor Five-Step (overview) | 10 |
| • The warm-up | 10 |
| • Introduce the subject | 20 |
| • Interview for needs, introduce benefits | 30 |
| • Make the request | 30 |
| • Close | 15 |
| G. Break | 15 |
| H. Solicitation role play | 40 |
| I. Fears, concerns, questions | 20 |
| J. Confidence builders and personal marketing goals | 15 |
| K. Review of assignments, timeline, and system of follow-up and support | 10 |
| L. Adjourn | 10 |

Total time: 5 hours

# Solicitor Training Guide

*15 minutes*

## A. Get settled, welcome, introductions, brief review, goals for the session

Open the session with a warm welcome and a big thank-you to the participants for playing the important role of Solicitor. Invite participants to introduce themselves and briefly share why being a part of the promotion campaign is important to them. (This question can be found on page 18 of the Pocket Guide.) Briefly review the purpose, goals, target audience, and timeline for the campaign and the role Solicitors will play in it. Pause for questions and answers. Then present goals for this session (listed in the agenda for this session).

If you have not already distributed the *Pocket Guide for Marketing Representatives*, do so at this time.

*10 minutes*

## B. Great solicitations

Ask participants to think of a time when they were on the *receiving end* of a great solicitation—whether for a nonprofit cause or a commercial interest. Ask a number of participants to tell a little about their experiences and what made them pleasant. Get as many examples out as quickly as possible, but don't encourage much discussion at this point. Make the point that the stereotype of solicitation as a negative experience often doesn't hold true—for either party involved.

*10 minutes*

## C. Know your prospects

Ask participants to take out their personal prospect lists or, if prospect lists aren't to be distributed until later, hand out a sample list. Explain how you identified the prospects and give as much general information about them as possible. Review how prospects have been or will be cultivated and how and when Solicitors will be involved. Note that individual background information is provided on each prospect and that more information will be made available when necessary. Facilitate a short discussion on what type of background information on prospects is helpful.

*30 minutes*

## D. The good, the bad, and the ugly

Divide participants into small groups of three or four people. Refer to the opening exercise on great solicitations as a starting point for the groups to discuss the good, bad, and ugly of solicitations. First ask participants to recall their positive receiving-end experiences and discuss why they responded well. Give groups ten minutes to discuss their answers and write them in the Pocket Guide on page 19. Ask for examples to share with the large group and list them.

Next ask participants to take ten minutes to think of negative experiences they have had, share "the bad and the ugly" in their small groups, and write these responses in the Pocket Guide under question 13, "What turns me off." Ask for examples to share with the large group and list them.

Close this portion by asking the group to what extent it believes Solicitors are responsible for the differences between the good, bad, and ugly. Use this as a segue into the skills-building portion of the agenda, "The Solicitor Five-Step."

## E. Break

*10 minutes*

## F. The Solicitor Five-Step

*10 minutes for overview*

Using an overhead transparency, introduce the five stages of a solicitation and refer participants to pages 20–26 of the Pocket Guide to follow along. Briefly describe the stages, reading each goal aloud.

**Stage 1: *The warm-up.*** Stage 1 is the hello-how-are-you stage. It can range from name, address, and serial number to a lengthy discussion of good fishing spots to actually packing off on a trip to one. The amount of warm-up required varies. Prospects run the gamut from those who consider warming up beside the point to those who'll never *get* to the point unless they're good and warm first.

*Goal: for prospects to feel at ease with you and with the pace of the conversation.*

**Stage 2: *Introduce the subject.*** Stage 2 is the let's-get-down-to-business stage. The Solicitor guides the conversation to the subject at hand, briefly introduces the solid purpose behind the promotion effort, and expresses hopes for a favorable response. Unless a prospect breaks in with questions, this is the only one-sided stage of solicitation.

*Goal: to make it clear what the coming conversation is about and convey your commitment to the organization or cause.*

**Stage 3: *Interview for needs, introduce benefits.*** Stage 3 is the let's-see-how-we-can-make-this-work-for-you stage. Ideally, it's a gabfest in which the *prospect* does most of the talking. The Solicitor listens and probes for ways to formulate a meaningful exchange that truly benefits the prospect. This is the most artful stage of solicitation.

*Goal: to learn what concerns or attracts prospects about the exchange, to offer reassurance if needed, and to present benefits prospects truly value.*

**Stage 4: *Make the request.*** Stage 4 is the well-here-we-go stage. The Solicitor pops the question in clear, direct, and respectful terms. The request may lead in a variety of directions—to Stage 3 for more discussion, to an opening to "upsell," to disappointment, or to champagne.

***Goal:*** *to directly ask the prospect to make a commitment, to discuss the request in any way the prospect wishes, and to move toward an agreement.*

**Stage 5: *Close.*** Stage 5 is the let's-come-to-an-agreement stage. The agreement is to one of three things: (1) a follow-up step to take the solicitation further; (2) a final "yes" on the part of the prospect; (3) a final no. Until what the Solicitor has heard as agreement has been restated and reinforced, there isn't a close. The Solicitor motto: no loose ends.

***Goal:*** *to come to a definite agreement and to leave the prospect feeling appreciated for whatever response they give.*

Following are directions for discussing each of these stages.

*10 minutes*

**Discussion of Stage 1: *The warm-up***

Once the stages are presented, facilitate a full group discussion of Stage 1. Ask participants what they can say and do to help prospects feel at ease. List their answers. As you elicit suggestions and write them on a flip chart, ask participants to write notes on Stage 1 in the Pocket Guide (page 20).

*20 minutes*

**Discussion of Stage 2: *Introduce the subject***

Ask participants to consider what they would say to a prospect to guide the conversation to the subject at hand—the purpose behind the promotion campaign. Then give participants five minutes to write a statement introducing the subject. Encourage them to refer to their previous Pocket Guide exercises, key messages, and other materials you have provided. Ask for two or three participants willing to present their statements to the large group and discuss the strengths and weaknesses of their approaches. Give each volunteer a round of applause.

Summarize by reminding participants that their statements should directly introduce the purpose of the solicitation—the prospect will be asked for something—should convey the organization's mission and results, and should come from the heart in terms of the Solicitor's own experience and values. Caution them not to turn it into a speech. Give participants five minutes to make notes in the Pocket Guide on the statements they will make. (Space for such notes is on page 21 of the Pocket Guide.)

**Discussion of Stage 3:** *Interview for needs, introduce benefits*     *30 minutes*

To begin discussion of Stage 3, emphasize the importance of being prepared to ask a series of *open-ended questions*. Use an overhead transparency as you go through the following examples:

- *What are you looking for in a [class . . . concert series . . . membership . . . degree program . . . set of materials . . . support group . . . ]?*
- *What would you most want out of it?*
- *What are your considerations in making a contribution?*
- *What has made you feel good about what you have supported in the past?*
- *When you've volunteered before, what made it a good experience?*
- *What would be rewarding to you in your relationship with our organization?*

Give participants five minutes to generate open-ended questions with a partner. Ask people to share the questions with the group while you list the questions on a flip chart. Give participants a few minutes to make notes on page 22 of the Pocket Guide, the "Open-ended questions" section.

To continue discussion on Stage 3, emphasize the importance of *listening to* and *honoring* prospects' concerns about the organization or project. Ask for examples of concerns they might hear from prospects and how they, as Solicitors, could respond to those concerns. Using an overhead transparency, cite the following as possible responses:

- *I'm so sorry that happened.*
- *That is certainly a valid concern. I'd like to tell you one thing that may help ease your concern . . . [list specifics].*
- *I understand those things did happen in the past. I think some changes have been made. Here they are . . . [list specifics].*
- *I will certainly pass that along to someone who can address it right away.*
- *I'll look into that and get back to you with more information.*

Encourage Solicitors to be sure to confirm the validity of prospects' experiences, to answer questions fully and honestly, to listen for concerns they can address with facts, and to avoid offering conflicting opinions that could lead to any kind of dispute. Then give participants two or three minutes to make notes on page 23 of the Pocket Guide, the "Responding to concerns" section.

Next, emphasize the importance of *reinforcing prospects' interests* and *values* by introducing benefits. Ask for examples of interests and values Solicitors might hear and how they could respond. Using an overhead transparency, cite the following as possible statements Solicitors might make:

- *I think you'll be very pleased with what we're offering . . . [list specifics].*

- *I want you to know how much [organization] is in line with your thinking. Funds are used for . . . [specifics]. Donors are kept informed by . . . [specifics]. Donors are invited to . . . [specifics]. As a donor you'll receive . . . [specifics].*

- *I'm so glad to hear you say that! I know volunteering with [organization] is a positive experience for similar reasons . . . [specifics].*

- *What you've said is so important and we're right with you. [Organization's] plans are to . . . [specifics].*

Encourage Solicitors to listen for real benefits you offer that provide value to your prospect and to reinforce these connections. Caution them not to exaggerate or make up anything they don't know for sure. Tell them to draw on their own knowledge of the organization or cause. Encourage them to study all the information you have provided and take it upon themselves to learn even more. Give participants two or three minutes to make notes in the Pocket Guide on page 23, the "Introducing benefits" section.

*30 minutes*

**Discussion of Stage 4: *Make the request***

To move into a discussion of Stage 4, break participants into small groups of three or four people and give them five minutes to brainstorm how they will make their requests. Explain the need to make a bridge from the needs and benefits discussion of Stage 3, but caution them to avoid elaborate build-ups before "popping the question." Use an overhead transparency to display and review the following examples:

- *May I put you down for season tickets for the family?*

- *The auction committee would like to request a donated one-year lease on a new car. Will that work for you?*

- *Would you like to fill out the preliminary enrollment form right now?*

- *Can I put you down for this month's volunteer orientation session?*

- *A contribution of any size you can afford would be much appreciated. Does $25 sound about right?*

- *We'd like you to be a Community Pacesetter. You'll be one of ten who make gifts of $100,000 or more. Is that a good level for you?*

After the small groups have brainstormed their own requests, ask them for their responses and list them on the flip chart. Remind Solicitors of the importance of being quiet for a moment once they have made the request. Give participants a few minutes to make notes on page 24 of the Pocket Guide, the "Making the request" section.

Next, explain how to respond to an initial negative or hesitant reply by asking additional open-ended questions. Present the following examples as you do so:

- *Would a different ticket package work better?*
- *What would work for you?*
- *Are there questions I can answer that would help you be ready?*
- *Is it a question of timing? Would another date be better?*
- *What does sound right?*
- *What is a good level for you?*
- *What's missing for you?*
- *I'm sorry to hear you say that. Can you tell me what's in the way for you?*

Ask for questions or discussion on responding to negative or hesitant replies and how Solicitors might move the prospect to a more positive position. This usually means returning to Stage 3 (interview for needs, introduce benefits), modifying the request, and asking again. Explain that no can indeed mean no and that Solicitors should graciously accept a negative response when this is the case. Give participants a few minutes to make notes on page 25 of the Pocket Guide, the "Handling negative or hesitating responses" section.

Next, introduce the concept of "upselling." Remind participants to immediately say "thank you" for a positive response, even if it isn't all they asked for. Explain that upselling is called for when they believe prospects may be willing to do a bit more if prompted. Solicitors may ask for a faster or larger commitment. In the large group, ask for examples of when participants have given an initial yes in a solicitation, but gone on to do more when prompted. Give participants a few minutes to make notes on page 25 in the Pocket Guide, the "Upselling" section.

### Discussion of Stage 5: *Close*                    *15 minutes*

Introduce Stage 5 by referring to a *close* as an end of the conversation that settles on one of three kinds of agreement: (1) a follow-up step to take the solicitation further; (2) a final yes from the prospect; or (3) a final no from the prospect. Give participants ten minutes in small groups of three or four people to talk through the three kinds of agreement they will reach, what they will actually say to clearly confirm agreement, and a few "dos and don'ts" for a close. In the large group, share "dos and don'ts," and then give participants a few minutes to make notes on page 26 of the Pocket Guide.

Finish this section with reminders to say "thank you" for whatever closing has happened, to complete any paperwork on the spot, and to follow up immediately on next steps and any necessary reporting in.

*15 minutes*      ## G. Break

*40 minutes*      ## H. Solicitation role play

Ask for volunteers to do a mock solicitation, one in the role of prospect, the other as Solicitor. Encourage them to use their notes and to attempt to cover all five stages in ten minutes. Be sure to applaud them; then facilitate a discussion of strengths and weaknesses in the solicitation. Repeat the exercise with several more pairs of volunteers.

*20 minutes*      ## I. Fears, concerns, questions

Give participants five minutes in pairs to identify their fears, concerns, and questions.

Share the answers in the large group and facilitate responses.

*15 minutes*      ## J. Confidence builders and personal marketing goals

Give participants five minutes to complete the statement "I will build my confidence by" on page 27 of the Pocket Guide. Share confidence-building ideas in the large group and encourage Solicitors to add more ideas to their own lists.

In this final training exercise, participants set personal marketing goals for their participation. In some campaigns, this means the actual share of your overall marketing goal that each person agrees to be responsible for and may even involve an assignment, a quota, or suggested target results. At the other end of the spectrum, personal marketing goals are strictly optional and may be as modest as "to get out there and give it a try." Explain how you want your Solicitors to approach the question; then ask them to write their goals on page 27 of the Pocket Guide. You may wish to complete this exercise by asking each Solicitor to state his or her goals aloud and give each person a round of cheers and applause.

## K. Review of assignments, timeline, and system of follow-up and support

*10 minutes*

Remind the Solicitors that they need to get going on their contacts immediately, and explain the timeline for getting responses to the coordinator. Explain how to report any feedback they get from their prospects, as well as any other information that might be important to the campaign. Respond to questions and point out the Solicitor tips on pages 34–37 of the Pocket Guide.

## L. Adjourn

*10 minutes*

Take a few minutes to bring things to a close, thank participants, and end on a high note with a motivational send-off.

## Total Solicitor training time: 5 hours

# Tips for Marketing Representatives

The following set of tips and reminders is also provided in the *Pocket Guide for Marketing Representatives.*

## Tips for All Marketing Representatives

### 1. Remember the mission.

In moments of shyness, discouragement, or if you're just darn tired, think of the mission and imagine its positive impact in just one setting with just one person. Say to yourself, "Whether or not this happens depends on me." Then take a deep breath and forge ahead.

### 2. Make an impression that would impress *you.*

Learn everything you can about your organization. Read, ask questions, go on tours, observe programs or classes, attend performances and events, talk with others involved. Reflect on what most deeply touches or impresses you. When you express *that*, your message will come through loud and clear.

### 3. Think the most of people.

Marketing lore is rich with tales of prospects outperforming initial expectations. Never get snagged by the "I'm-sure-they-can't" syndrome. The last thing you want to learn is that someone would have said yes, or done more, if only they'd been asked.

### 4. Take no for an answer.

There are times when no means "not that much" or "not this month" or "never mind the party invitation, just get to the bottom line." Don't be afraid to ask a follow-up question, but if the answer is really no, then graciously accept it.

### 5. Say "thank you."

Sincerely and often. Thank people for their interest, for taking the time to talk with you, for coming to an event, for their consideration, for helping you along the way, for saying yes. Thank those who come through in big and small ways with equal enthusiasm. Thank *yourself* for all you are doing!

## Tips for Ambassadors

### 1. Listen more than you speak.

Whenever you give people the chance to express their interests and opinions, you go a long way toward creating an exchange relationship. Listen for opportunities to begin a conversation, for personal connections, for ways to ask follow-up questions. The glow of good conversation is brightest when we feel we have been heard.

### 2. Accentuate the positive.

In general, people are more attracted to stories of progress and positive results than grim statistics and warnings of impending doom. There is certainly a place for the hard, cold facts, but it rarely serves your aim to have people walk away depressed.

### 3. Be contagious.

Don't be afraid to let your light shine through. Studies show the impression we leave is based far more on our tone of voice and body language than on what we actually say. Remember, what you've got is catching.

### 4. Confirm a possible next step.

When someone has expressed openness or interest in the right direction, be sure to set the stage for a next step. In nearly any setting, it is appropriate to exchange business cards or take down a phone number and address. Confirm that written information will be sent or that another form of contact will occur. Then make sure whatever follow-up you have promised happens right away.

## Tips for Door-Openers

### 1. Be judicious.

It's one thing to sparingly unlock your address book and provide names and information about your colleagues, family, and friends. Opening a side business as a mailing list broker is quite another. Golden rule: Promote unto others as you would have them promote unto you.

### 2. Give a strong personal endorsement.

When making introductions, tell people how strong you feel about the cause. Let them know you think it's great and why. Express your hope that they'll appreciate the importance of the mission as much as you do.

### 3. Be visible.

If your contacts are being invited to a performance, an open house, or any type of presentation or event you can possibly attend, try to be there to welcome them. Whenever you can, personally introduce your contacts to organizational leaders and others whose expertise or interests match theirs.

## Tips for Cultivators

### 1. Show 'em a good time.

Some people will give you ten minutes in their office; others yearn to be wined and dined. Successful cultivation means knowing your soil. Gear plans to the audience, be a first-rate host, make strategic introductions, and attend to everything you can think of to make your invitations touted as good ones to accept.

### 2. Mix and match.

Think creatively about who to invite to what. This may mean suggesting just the right Solicitor to come along to lunch or inviting an unusual cross-section of party guests. People watching, networking, and socializing are all bona-fide benefits to your prospects.

### 3. Expect to be popular.

Like Door-Openers, it's important to remember that cultivation is a two-way street. Your prospects will likely return the favor with a future invitation of their own.

## Tips for Solicitors

### 1. Let the prospect set the pace.

The amount of time you spend in each stage of a direct solicitation will vary based on the personal preferences and cultural background of your prospect. You are in charge of moving things along, but take your cues from your prospect.

### 2. Let them know you care.

You do get to do some of the talking. "Bob, I've had the chance to visit with some of those kids down at the Center and I know what it means for them. I really believe we're changing lives." Now who can resist that?

### 3. Encourage them to do the talking.

Any experienced salesperson will tell you the more the prospect does the talking the more likely a sale is in the offing. From time to time, a dream prospect comes along: "Well, I guess we both know why we're here. Here's what I'd like to do. I want to be much more generous this year. . . ." For the most part, you'll have to pose open-ended questions and perhaps use some of the following prompts to hear more:

- *Can you tell me more about that?*
- *What do you mean when you say . . . ?*
- *What's an example of that?*
- *I'd like to know more about your thinking on that issue.*
- *I'm not sure I understand how you are using the word . . . .*
- *You started to say something about . . . .*
- *You mentioned something about . . . .*

### 4. Never get into a dispute.

Prospects sometimes use solicitation time to air grievances, to share their philosophies on the state of the world, or even to be deliberately provocative. Listen respectfully. Offer objective, fact-based points of view and answer questions honestly and directly. Once they've got it off their chest or they've seen you don't wither under fire, things tend to take a turn for the better.

### 5. Ask for the exchange.

For some Solicitors, this is the hardest part of the job. You may want to practice in the mirror to get used to hearing yourself ask for an exchange. This one's strictly in your court. Make it simple and to the point. Remember that the mission of your organization is what this exchange is all about. Then ask for a commitment.

## 6. Upsell.

If you had trouble asking for an exchange, this one's really going to get you. Let's practice. She comes right out and pledges $400. Leadership Circle is just $100 more. You say, "Thank you, Li, that's wonderful! I just want you to know Leadership Circle gifts begin at $500. Would you like to consider that level?" There. That's not so hard.

## 7. Don't forget to close!

It ain't over 'til it's over. Never assume you've reached agreement until you formally close the solicitation. You'd be amazed at the number of Solicitors who've had such great conversations, they just plumb forget!

## 8. Don't worry about doing it perfectly.

It's not a matter of ticking off the stages. Solicitation is a real conversation with a real person. Relax and be yourself. That will carry you farther than doing it absolutely by the book . . . this one included.

## 9. If at first you don't succeed . . .

. . . you're normal, unless you're the enviable superstar who bats a thousand. Most of us need to take a few strikeouts in stride, keep refining our technique, and keep stepping up to the plate. In part, it's a numbers game. Keep trying and you're bound to score.

## 10. Say "thank you."

In the rare event you were about to forget.

# Worksheets

**SECTION 1—Purpose**

Complete this worksheet to determine the *purpose* of your promotion effort.

1. Describe the situation or need your effort will address. Are you pursuing long-term goals? Has a serious problem suddenly developed? Are there new opportunities to take advantage of?

2. Describe the types of resources, support, or response your promotion effort will produce.

3. Describe how your organization's capabilities or skills will be enhanced by the effort. What will people learn? How might your organization be changed for the better?

## SECTION 2A—Participants

In Step 4, you will list each individual you plan to recruit for your promotion effort. At this point, it is only necessary to identify what groups these people may come from and the approximate number of potential marketing representatives in each.

**Group**                          **Number of potential marketing representatives**

A. Staff

B. Board

C. Standing committees or auxiliaries

D. Existing or new volunteers

E. Current members, program
   participants, or customers

F. Other groups

**SECTION 2B—Participants**

Decide who should serve on the Marketing Task Force. The group ideally includes
six to twelve people.

A. Brainstorm a list of all potential Task Force participants.

B. Put a (circle) around the names of those you believe will be best and who, as a group,
   satisfy these criteria:

   • At least one participant in Step 1: Define the Scope

   • Representatives from groups who will later be asked to participate

   • Individuals with an understanding of marketing, communications, and solicitation

   • A representative from the board

   • A representative from upper management

   • Others who can help move the effort forward

   • Potential chair or cochairs

C. Put a rectangle around backup names in case those you first ask to join the Task Force
   are unavailable.

**SECTION 3—Timeline**

A. If you already have a deadline for your effort, write it below.

If the timeline for your effort is flexible, or you want to check the feasibility of your current deadline, use the exercise below.

B. Using the steps in this book as a guide, look ahead, note the major components you expect may be included in your marketing effort, and estimate amounts of time needed. Start with Step 2, Form a Marketing Task Force.

| Component | Amount of time to accomplish |
|---|---|
| Step 2: Form a Marketing Task Force | |
| Step 3: Set goals; define targeting, message, and communications strategies | |
| Step 4: Determine roles, people to involve, and recruitment techniques | |
| Step 5: Develop a master timeline and action plan for the effort | |
| Step 6: Implement the recruitment plan | |
| Step 7: Hold motivational training | |
| Step 8: Provide ongoing follow-up and support | |
| Step 9: Reward, recognize, reenlist | |
| Step 10: Celebrate success and evaluate the effort | |

C. What would be the ideal deadline for the purpose of your promotion effort to be achieved?

**SECTION 3—Timeline**

D. Working backward from the deadline, does it appear you have enough time to accomplish the major components of the effort?

E. If not, how can the deadline be extended or the timeline compressed?

F. Set your timeline:

Our Task Force will begin work by:

Our promotion effort will be completed by:

**SECTION 4—Address Budget Issues**

A. Our ballpark cost estimate for the promotion campaign is:

If making an estimate is not yet possible, the next steps provide guidance.

B. Funds already available for the effort:

| **Source** | **Amount** |
| --- | --- |
| | |
| | |
| | |
| | |
| | |
| | |
| | |

C. Our plan for additional funds:

| **Potential Source** | **Amount** | **How to Obtain** |
| --- | --- | --- |
| | | |
| | | |
| | | |
| | | |
| | | |
| | | |
| | | |

## SECTION 1—The Task Force Charge Statement

The Task Force mission is:

*To plan, help implement, and evaluate a people-to-people promotion campaign.*

Summarize Worksheet 1 to complete A–D below; then go on to respond to Points E and F.

A. The purpose and—if they are already set—the goals of the promotion effort:

B. Groups expected to participate:

C. An overall timeline with major check-in points:

*(continued)*

## SECTION 1—The Task Force Charge Statement

D. A budget or expectations to create one; sources of funds or a funding plan:

E. Parameters that specify any absolute "dos" or "don'ts":

(For example, "Do honor our new diversity plan." "Don't schedule any event within two weeks of the annual meeting.")

F. A "point person" or group to whom the Task Force is responsible:

## SECTION 2A—Recruit a Chair or Cochairs

List and prioritize possible candidates to chair or cochair the Marketing Task Force.

The executive director or board chair will:

☐ Meet with prospective chair or cochairs

☐ Go over the scope and charge statement with them

☐ Extend the invitation

☐ Gain acceptance

Date by which Task Force chair is to be recruited: _____

## SECTION 2B—Recruit the Marketing Task Force

Look back over the list of prospective Task Force members from Worksheet 1, Section 2B (page 137).

1. Discuss the list, make additions or deletions, and finalize it.

2. Possible dates for a first meeting of the Task Force:

3. The point person and Task Force chair will:

☐ Decide who should meet with prospective members

☐ Go over the scope and charge statement with prospective members

☐ Extend the invitation

☐ Gain acceptance

☐ Poll for availability on first meeting dates

☐ Inform Task Force members of date and time for first meeting

☐ Make a final list of names, addresses, telephone numbers, fax numbers, and E-mail addresses for distribution at the first Task Force meeting

## SECTION 1—Set Marketing Goals

In what categories will you set marketing goals?

- ☐ Funding
- ☐ Volunteer recruitment
- ☐ Participation in programs, services, or events
- ☐ Enrollment

- ☐ Membership
- ☐ Sales of tickets, books, services, or other items
- ☐ In-kind contributions
- ☐ Other: _____

Use the following process to set your specific marketing goals.

Responses to questions 1–3 below should be brainstormed: that is, every answer is acceptable, even if they conflict.

The group should attempt to reach general agreement on question 4. You may have one or more goal categories. Make copies of this worksheet and repeat these steps for *each* goal you want to set.

**1. What are the *ideal* results we could achieve?**

First, define the categories of exchanges you want to make: funds, volunteers, members, in-kind contributions, and so forth, as listed in the columns at the top of this worksheet. Within each category you may have more than one goal. For example, if your goal category is funding, you might want specific results in major gifts, direct mail, and foundation grants. You might have a second goal category of in-kind contributions, with results specified in supplies, raffle prize donations, and computers.

Now think big: if everything goes perfectly, what could the results be? (A little dreaming is fine at this point.)

| Goal category | Ideal results (how much of what by when) |
|---|---|
|  |  |
|  |  |
|  |  |
|  |  |

*(continued)*

## SECTION 1—Set Marketing Goals

2. **What argues in favor of our ability to achieve these ideal results?**

   Think about factors inside the organization as well as those outside.

   | *Inside* factors working for us | *Outside* factors working for us |
   |---|---|
   | | |
   | | |
   | | |
   | | |
   | | |
   | | |

3. **What argues against our ability to achieve these results?**

   Now think about factors, inside and outside, that might hold you back.

   | *Inside* factors working against us | *Outside* factors working against us |
   |---|---|
   | | |
   | | |
   | | |
   | | |
   | | |
   | | |

**SECTION 1—Set Marketing Goals**

4. **What are our realistic, achievable goals? By when?**

   Try for consensus on this question.

   A. Reflect on the internal and external factors, and then take a quick "gut-response" poll.

   B. Discuss people's gut responses and attempt to arrive at a consensus. If you can't agree, draft low-end and high-end goals for now.

   | Achievable goal | By when |
   |---|---|
   |  |  |
   |  |  |
   |  |  |
   |  |  |
   |  |  |
   |  |  |

## SECTION 2A—Segment Your Target Audience into Distinct Groups

Using the list of segment characteristics provided on page 34 as a guide, brainstorm a list of all groups or individuals who could be segments of your target audience. Repeat this exercise for each goal you have set.

**Goal:**

Example: *70 participants in children's drama workshops by June 1*

**Target audience segments:**

- *Previous participants*
- *Siblings of previous participants*
- *Friends of previous participants*
- *Children of staff, board members, and volunteers*
- *Children who live in the neighborhood*
- *Hispanic children*
- *Children of parents who work in the arts*
- *Children of parents who purchase tickets to arts events*
- *Other recreational children's programs in the area*
- *Participants in music and drama programs in schools, religious organizations, and community groups*

**Goal:**


**Target audience segments:**

_____

_____

_____

_____

_____

_____

_____

_____

**SECTION 2A—Segment Your Target Audience into Distinct Groups**

Goal:

Target audience segments:

_____

_____

_____

_____

_____

_____

_____

_____

_____

_____

_____

Test your lists and strike out any groups that do not meet at least one of the following criteria:

- Capacity to make exchanges in line with our goals
- Making exchanges would be desirable to us
- They stand to benefit
- They may have an interest in making exchanges with us

## SECTION 2B—Target Groups to Approach: Prioritize the Segments

For each goal, recopy below the final list of market segments you brainstormed and tested on Worksheet 3, Section 2A. (Make copies of this worksheet as needed.) In the following exercise, estimate what portion of your overall goal each segment could produce. Rate each segment using the following formula:

$$\frac{\text{Capacity or Desirability}}{\text{Difficulty}}$$

Each segment receives one of the following ratings: $\frac{\text{High}}{\text{Low}}$   $\frac{\text{High}}{\text{High}}$   $\frac{\text{Low}}{\text{Low}}$   or   $\frac{\text{Low}}{\text{High}}$

Based on ratings, assign each segment to the *A-*, *B-*, or *C-list* and estimate each segment's capacity: **A-list:** $\frac{\text{High}}{\text{Low}}$ or $\frac{\text{High}}{\text{High}}$   **B-list:** $\frac{\text{Low}}{\text{Low}}$   **C-list:** $\frac{\text{Low}}{\text{High}}$

*Example:*

| Segment | Rating | A-, B-, or C-List | Could Produce |
|---|---|---|---|
| • *Previous participants* | $\frac{High}{Low}$ | *A* | *50* |
| • *Hispanic children* | $\frac{High}{High}$ | *A* | *15* |
| • *Participants in music and drama programs in schools, religious organizations, and community groups* | $\frac{Low}{Low}$ | *B* | *5* |
| • *Children of parents who purchase tickets to arts events* | $\frac{Low}{High}$ | *C* | *0* |

Once you have rated each segment and estimated its capacity, you can verify whether your goals appear realistic and achievable—or perhaps too modest.

Our draft goal is: _____

Total estimated amount all segments could produce: _____

Our goal is: ☐ Verified     ☐ Too high     ☐ Too low

You have now affirmed a draft goal or made a case to increase or decrease it. At this point, the Task Force should come to final consensus on one or more goals.

**Our realistic and achievable goal is:** _____

**SECTION 2B—Target Groups to Approach: Prioritize the Segments**

| Segment | Rating | A-, B-, or C-List | Could Produce |
|---|---|---|---|
| | | | |
| | | | |
| | | | |
| | | | |
| | | | |
| | | | |
| | | | |
| | | | |
| | | | |
| | | | |
| | | | |
| | | | |
| | | | |

Once you have rated each segment and estimated its capacity, you can verify whether your goals appear realistic and achievable—or perhaps too modest.

Our draft goal is: _____

Total estimated amount all segments could produce: _____

Our goal is: ☐ Verified    ☐ Too high    ☐ Too low

You have now affirmed a draft goal or made a case to increase or decrease it. At this point, the Task Force should come to final consensus on one or more goals.

**Our realistic and achievable goal is:** _____

## SECTION 3A—Key Messages: Set Criteria

Judging the outcome of creative processes becomes manageable when you have a predefined taste test.

**Criteria we will use to judge draft messages:**
MUST include: *Tells people what we want them to think, feel, and do.*

**Additional criteria:**

## SECTION 3B—Key Messages: Develop Factual Content

The factual content of your message should plainly tell your target audience why your organization or cause is worthy of support, what particular needs *they* have that your organization can address, and how you want them to respond. To develop draft factual content, answer these five questions:

A. What needs of our target market do we address?

B. Why is what we do important to them?

C. How can we describe what we do so it's easy for others to understand?

D. Who benefits from what we do and how do they benefit?

E. What do we want people to think, feel, and do?

**SECTION 3C—Key Messages: Identify Resistance and Receptivity**

In this exercise, you identify potential resistance to your message. From the perspective of your target audiences, do you face communications barriers because of:

- Inaccurate perceptions of the organization, its programs, or the general field of work in which the organization is involved?

- Negative associations with the organization, its programs, or the general field of work?

- Hostile or antagonistic attitudes?

- Uninformed or negative assumptions?

- Ways in which the organization's image is tarnished?

- A very crowded marketplace or "compassion fatigue"?

- Other barriers?

**Potential resistance to our messages:**

## SECTION 3C—Key Messages: Identify Resistance and Receptivity

Now go on to identify potential receptivity to your message. From the standpoint of your target audiences, do you face communications advantages because of:

- Accurate and positive perceptions of the organization, its programs, or the organization's general field of work?

- Helpful media attention?

- Market segments actively seeking exchanges with you?

- High demand or enthusiastic support for what you offer?

- Being seen as a leader or change agent?

- Awards and formal recognition your organization has received?

- Other advantages?

**Potential receptivity for our messages:**

## SECTION 3D—Key Messages: Develop Emotional Content

Effective messages strike a chord with both head and heart. In this exercise, you develop emotional content for your message by recording Task Force members' responses to the following questions:

A. What aspects of the organization's work have most touched or affected you? Why?

B. In what way do you experience meaning in our organization's mission?

C. What is the most compelling reason someone should support our organization?

Review the above responses and:

- Underline recurring themes.
- Circle words or phrases that especially hit home for the group.

## SECTION 3E—Draft Key Messages

Writers, editors, or group who will draft key messages:

Deadline for drafts: _____

Drawing on the raw material generated on Worksheet 3, Sections 3A–3D, draft key messages in four forms as follows:

A. *Case statement*: A relatively short statement—two to four paragraphs—that pulls together the who, what, when, where, why, and how of the organization's mission and the purpose behind the promotion campaign.

B. *Results of our mission*: Several succinct points showing your organization's positive results and accomplishments.

*(continued)*

**SECTION 3E—Draft Key Messages**

C. *Slogan or tag line* (or both): One or two short, memorable phrases that capture the essence of the case statement.

*For example:*

> **American Lung Association**
> Your first source of information for
> healthy lungs, smoking prevention, and clean air.     ← slogan
>
> *When you can't breathe, nothing else matters.*     ← tagline

D. *Persuasive statements*: Actual phrases or sentences marketing representatives can use when talking with prospects.

## SECTION 4—Choose Communications Materials and Techniques

A marketing and communications professional should play a central role in helping choose and conceptualize communications materials and techniques. Following is a list of options for basic materials to directly support marketing representatives. Use these to help you outline your communications strategy.

☐ Key messages: case statement, slogan or tag line, persuasive statements, examples of results

☐ Fact sheet

☐ Brochure

☐ Information packet

☐ Presentation overheads

☐ Presentation scripts

☐ Direct response materials

☐ Letterhead and thank-you notes

☐ At least one gimmick: (describe)

☐ Audiovisual tools: video, slide, or computer-based presentation

☐ Other: _____

_____

_____

_____

_____

_____

Materials and techniques to back up in-person promotion efforts:

☐ Public relations tools such as a master news release and set of background materials

☐ Advertising copy

☐ Media relations

☐ Special events

☐ Public speaking

☐ Telemarketing

☐ Partnerships or sponsorships

☐ Web page

☐ Other:

☐ Number and type of cultivation events:

_____

_____

_____

_____

_____

_____

_____

_____

## SECTION 5—Affirm Goals and Strategies

The Marketing Task Force now steps back to make sure the whole picture fits together. The following four questions help affirm the goals and strategies set by the Task Force.

A. Taken together, can your priority segments produce the results you want—do your goals hold up as realistic and achievable?

☐ Yes ☐ No

If not, revise your goals (down or up). Some groups like "stretch goals"—goals set just above what they feel is realistic in order to spark hard work. This can be effective as long as all involved agree on what is realistic and achievable and treat anything above as a true bonus. Otherwise you risk actual success being viewed as something less.

Affirmed or revised goals:

B. Do the targeting, key message, and communications strategies clearly build on one another? Do the strategies feel *doable?*

☐ Yes ☐ No

If not, identify potential changes in your strategies:

**SECTION 5—Affirm Goals and Strategies**

C. Does the effort hold together from a cost/benefit standpoint? Are budget estimates in line with available or attainable funds?

☐ Yes      ☐ No

If not, determine how you might reduce costs, and then identify any remaining financial gap. You will address overall funding for your effort in Step 5.

D. Do the strategies give the Task Force a sense of confidence and momentum?

☐ Yes      ☐ No

If strong reservations come up, stop and take stock. Adjust the strategies as needed. If you run up against problems you can't solve, seek expert advice.

## SECTION 1—Determine Roles

A. Determine needed roles and the approximate number of marketing representatives you will recruit for each.

☐ **Ambassadors**

No limit to the number who can play the role.

Goal for number of Ambassadors to recruit: _____

☐ **Door-Openers**

Will you need a significant number of introductions to get inside doors?

Goal for number of Door-Openers to recruit: _____

☐ **Cultivators**

Your communications strategy defines numbers of cultivation events (Worksheet 3, Section 4). How many Cultivators will that require?

Goal for number of Cultivators to recruit: _____

☐ **Solicitors**

Look back at your target audiences (Worksheet 3, Section 2B).

Approximately how many people will you solicit?

How many prospects per solicitor?

What about additional solicitors willing to make just one or two calls?

Goal for number of Solicitors to recruit: _____

*(continued)*

## SECTION 1—Determine Roles

B. Create a list of prospective marketing representatives with enough names to enable you to meet your goals for each marketing representative role. Remember, not everyone will say yes, so be sure to come up with a few extra names. Also, some names may appear for more than one role.

**Ambassadors:** (tend to be listed in groups)

**Door-Openers:**

## SECTION 1—Determine Roles

**Cultivators:**

**Solicitors:**

Review the number of prospective marketing representatives you have listed for each role and assess whether you have a sufficient number. If not, determine if you can:

- Add more potential marketing representatives to the list

- Ask some people to do more

- Extend your timeline, find efficiencies, or make other adjustments to compensate

- Consider the possibility of more modest goals

*(continued)*

**SECTION 1—Determine Roles**

C. Identify the names of people who will recruit your marketing representatives:

D. Once you have completed A, B, and C above, go back to Question B and assign each group or individual to a particular recruiter. Then create lists for each recruiter with names and contact information for the individuals and groups they are to contact.

Contact information:

- Name
- Address
- Phone, FAX, E-mail
- Potential role(s):  ☐ Ambassador     ☐ Door-Opener     ☐ Cultivator     ☐ Solicitor

## SECTION 2—Develop Mini-Job Descriptions

Use the following format to develop brief job descriptions for the four marketing representative roles. Also create descriptions for the chair or cochairs, if such positions exist.

**Organization name:**

**Goals of the effort:**

**Role:**

**Responsibilities:**

**Approximate number of contacts to be made (for Cultivators and Solicitors):** _____

**Beginning and ending dates of participation:** _____

**Number of training sessions and meetings to attend:** _____

## SECTION 1—Develop an Overall Calendar and Schedule for Production

### A. Overall calendar for the promotion campaign

| Step | Responsible | Begin | End | Budget |
|---|---|---|---|---|
| 1. Identification and training of recruiters | | | | |
| 2. Recruitment of marketing representatives | | | | |
| 3. Motivational training sessions | | | | |
| 4. Promotion campaign kickoff | | | | |
| 5. Special events: (list) | | | | |
| | | | | |
| | | | | |
| | | | | |
| | | | | |
| 6. Other events already on the calendar that can be coordinated with the promotion campaign: | | | | |
| | | | | |
| | | | | |
| | | | | |
| | | | | |
| 7. Phases: | | | | |
|   A. Advance solicitation | | | | |
|   B. Cultivation presentations and events | | | | |
|   C. Direct mail | | | | |
|   D. Full-scale solicitation | | | | |
|   E. Telemarketing | | | | |
|   F. Other: | | | | |
| | | | | |
| | | | | |
| 8. Check-in points or meetings for marketing representatives | | | | |
| 9. Campaign ends | | | | |
| 10. Celebration | | | | |
| 11. Evaluation | | | | |

      *(continued)*

## SECTION 1—Develop an Overall Calendar and Schedule for Production

### B. Production schedule

On Worksheet 3, Section 4, you identified the potential elements of your communications strategy. Now you will set a schedule for production and identify a communications coordinator.

1. To set the schedule for production, determine what set of materials and techniques you will use, who is responsible for each element, who needs to review and approve them, budgets, and, based on the master calendar, the deadline for each element to be ready.

| Tool/Technique | Responsible | Review/Approve | Budget | By When |
|---|---|---|---|---|
| | | | | |
| | | | | |
| | | | | |
| | | | | |
| | | | | |
| | | | | |
| | | | | |
| | | | | |
| | | | | |
| | | | | |
| | | | | |

2. Who can approve budget changes, if necessary? _____

3. Communications coordinator: _____

## SECTION 2—Outline the Training Effort

A. Set definite dates, times, and preferred locations for the training sessions and determine who from the campaign leadership will be there to greet participants. Give each session a title based on its role content (for example, *Ambassador Training; Solicitor Follow-up*).

| Session type | Date | Time | Location | Greeter |
|---|---|---|---|---|
|  |  |  |  |  |
|  |  |  |  |  |
|  |  |  |  |  |
|  |  |  |  |  |
|  |  |  |  |  |
|  |  |  |  |  |
|  |  |  |  |  |
|  |  |  |  |  |
|  |  |  |  |  |

B. Trainers or presenters from inside the organization:

C. Potential outside trainers or presenters:

D. Motivational training coordinator: _____

## SECTION 3—Assign Tasks for Follow-up and Support

A. Determine what individuals or teams will handle each aspect of follow-up and support:

| Task | Responsible |
|---|---|
| 1. Maintain a master list of all marketing representatives, their assigned prospects, and their progress. | |
| 2. Route new prospects to marketing representatives. | |
| 3. Make reminder calls. | |
| 4. Provide reassurance, support, and problem-solving help to marketing representatives. | |
| 5. Handle RSVPs. | |
| 6. Handle meeting and event arrangements. | |
| 7. Issue thank-yous and other acknowledgments. | |
| 8. Issue interim and final reports. | |
| 9. Be a liaison to the communications coordinator. | |
| 10. Provide other administrative support. | |

B. Follow-up and support coordinator: _____

**SECTION 4—Plan Rewards and Recognition**

A. Brainstorm ideas for how you will frequently remind marketing representatives of the value and importance of their efforts. (Circle) the ideas you like best and discuss how you will implement them.

    1. Ideas:

    2. Implementation:

*(continued)*

**SECTION 4—Plan Rewards and Recognition**

B. Follow the same process as above for tangible rewards (lunches, flowers, and so forth).

1. Ideas:

2. Implementation:

3. Set a rewards budget:

**SECTION 4—Plan Rewards and Recognition**

C. Brainstorm ideas for "standard" recognition items you will give to marketing representatives (plaques, certificates, and so forth). (Circle) the ideas you like best and discuss how you will implement them. The recognition coordinator should pull together ideas for individualized recognition as the effort progresses.

1. Ideas:

2. Implementation:

3. Set a recognition budget:

D. Rewards, recognition, and reenlistment coordinator: _____

**SECTION 5—Assign Celebration and Evaluation Coordinators**

A. Celebration coordinator: _____

B. Evaluation coordinator: _____

## SECTION 1—Recruitment Coordinator Checklist

This checklist serves as a recruitment to-do list for coordinators. The format allows for setting dates, recording progress, and noting additional details or steps.

| Step | Dates | Notes |
|---|---|---|
| **1. Schedule a mini-training session** | | |
| ☐ Presenters/trainers confirmed | | |
| ☐ Date, time, and place set | | |
| ☐ Invitations out | | |
| ☐ Follow-up calls made (as needed) | | |
| ☐ Responses in | | |
| **2. Organize recruitment lists** | | |
| ☐ Lists for individual recruiters ready | | |
| **3. Gather and finalize materials** | | |
| ☐ Distributed in advance: | | |
|   ☐ Written summary of the background, purpose, and goals of the marketing effort | | |
|   ☐ Key messages: case statement, slogan or tag line, persuasive statements, examples of results | | |
|   ☐ Mini-job descriptions | | |
|   ☐ Individual recruitment lists | | |
| ☐ Ready for training session: | | |
|   ☐ Recruitment letter | | |
|   ☐ Phone scripts, presentation scripts, or both | | |
|   ☐ Overhead transparencies | | |
|   ☐ Other: | | |

*(continued)*

**SECTION 1—Recruitment Coordinator Checklist**

| Step | Dates | Notes |
|---|---|---|
| **4. Plan the training session** | | |
| ☐ Agenda set | | |
| ☐ Location(s) confirmed | | |
| ☐ Logistics finalized | | |
|    ☐ Room(s) checked for size, seating, audiovisual capabilities | | |
|    ☐ Refreshments or meals planned | | |
|    ☐ Decorations, posters, displays arranged | | |
|    ☐ Presentation materials finalized | | |
|       ☐ Overheads | | |
|       ☐ Other audiovisual materials | | |
|    ☐ Flip chart and audiovisual equipment ordered | | |
|    ☐ Name tags ready | | |
|    ☐ Materials organized for easy distribution | | |
|    ☐ Additional festive touches | | |
|    ☐ Recruitment lists and other reference materials ready | | |
| ☐ Presenters and trainers ready | | |
| ☐ Plan in place for getting training information to those unable to attend | | |

**SECTION 1—Recruitment Coordinator Checklist**

| Step | Dates | Notes |
|---|---|---|
| **5. Follow up with recruiters** | | |
| ☐ Question-and-answer sheet prepared and distributed | | |
| ☐ Training information to recruiters who did not attend | | |
| ☐ Midpoint check-ins completed | | |
| ☐ Post-deadline follow-up completed | | |
| **6. Thank you and wrap-up** | | |
| ☐ Recruiters thanked | | |
| ☐ Results tabulated | | |
| ☐ Final list of marketing representatives prepared | | |
| **7. Prepare individualized prospect lists** | | |
| ☐ Prospect assignment session scheduled | | |
| ☐ Prospect lists completed | | |
| ☐ Lists forwarded to motivational training coordinators | | |
| **8. Evaluation** | | |
| ☐ Evaluation session scheduled | | |
| ☐ Evaluation completed | | |
| ☐ Success is marked | | |

## SECTION 2—Prospect List

On the next page include names of groups and individuals, contact information, and brief notes on each prospect that will be helpful to your marketing representatives. Make as many copies of this worksheet as needed.

**Prospect List Format**

Marketing representative name:

Organization name:

Promotion campaign slogan or tag line:

Overall goals:

Capsule description of the promotion effort:

Overall target audience:

Priority segments:

## SECTION 2—Prospect List

| Prospect | Deadline to contact | Deadline to report in |
|---|---|---|
| Organizations/groups to contact for presentations: | | |
| Individuals for personal contact: | | |

## SECTION 3—Evaluate the Recruitment Effort

Hold a Marketing Task Force meeting to answer these evaluation questions.

A. Did we achieve our recruitment goals?

B. If not, what did we misjudge or fail to foresee?

C. Did the recruitment process go smoothly?

D. What have we learned that will help us as we go on?

E. Do we need to revise any part of our plans?

F. If we judge our recruitment effort a success, how should we celebrate it?

## Checklist for Motivational Training Coordinators

| Step | Dates | Notes |
|------|-------|-------|
| **1. Finalize schedule of training sessions**<br>☐ Presenters/trainers confirmed<br>☐ Dates, times, and places set<br>☐ Follow-up calls made (as needed)<br>☐ Participation confirmed | | |
| **2. Gather and finalize materials**<br>☐ Distributed in advance:<br>  ☐ Written summary of the background, purpose, and goals of your marketing effort<br>  ☐ Key messages: case statement, results, slogan or tag line, persuasive statements<br>  ☐ Sample communications pieces<br>  ☐ Individual prospect lists (Solicitor training)<br>  ☐ Confirmation letter<br>☐ Ready for training session:<br>  ☐ Agenda<br>  ☐ Copies of *Pocket Guide for Marketing Representatives*<br>  ☐ Phone or presentation scripts<br>  ☐ Communications materials to be used by marketing representatives<br>  ☐ Follow-up and report forms (Door-Opener and Cultivator training) | | |

*(continued)*

## Checklist for Motivational Training Coordinators

| Step | Dates | Notes |
| --- | --- | --- |

### 3. Plan session agendas

☐ Agendas set

☐ Plan in place to get training information to those unable to attend sessions

### 4. Handle logistics

☐ Location(s) confirmed

☐ Room(s) checked for size, seating, audiovisual capabilities

☐ Refreshments or meals planned

☐ Decorations, posters, displays arranged

☐ Presentation materials finalized:

   ☐ Overheads

   ☐ Other audiovisual materials

☐ Flip chart and audiovisual equipment ordered

☐ Background music chosen

☐ Welcome table planned and staffed

☐ Name tags ready

☐ Materials organized for easy distribution

☐ Additional festive touches in place

☐ Reference materials ready:

   ☐ Master prospect list

   ☐ Unassigned prospect list

## Checklist for Motivational Training Coordinators

| Step | Dates | Notes |
|---|---|---|
| **5. Follow up with absentees** | | |
| ☐ Training information to marketing representatives unable to attend sessions | | |
| **6. Thank representatives and wrap up the process** | | |
| ☐ Marketing representatives thanked for attending | | |
| ☐ Those who organized, presented, or helped with training thanked | | |
| ☐ Individualized prospect lists finalized | | |
| ☐ Final lists passed on to follow-up and support coordinator | | |
| **7. Gather evaluation feedback** | | |
| ☐ Small sample contacted for feedback | | |
| ☐ Summary written up for later use | | |

## Checklist for Follow-up and Support Coordinators

| Step | Dates | Notes |
|---|---|---|
| **1. Orient follow-up and support team** | | |
| ☐ Team members identified | | |
| ☐ Meeting scheduled to go over systems and responsibilities | | |
| **2. Master list of prospects** | | |
| ☐ System for maintaining master list of prospects determined; master list created | | |
| ☐ Progress, additions, new assignments, and reassignments are being tracked | | |
| **3. Routing** | | |
| ☐ Routing system determined | | |
| ☐ Follow-up calls made to marketing representatives on prospect identification, assignment, and activity forms | | |
| ☐ Calls made on forms not yet returned | | |
| ☐ Marketing representative questions are being answered promptly | | |
| ☐ New prospects are being routed effectively | | |
| ☐ Customer feedback is being conveyed for follow-up | | |
| **4. Reminders** | | |
| ☐ System for reminders determined | | |
| ☐ Routine check-ins occurring | | |
| ☐ Aggressive follow-up occurring when necessary | | |

*(continued)*

## Checklist for Follow-up and Support Coordinators

| Step | Dates | Notes |
|------|-------|-------|
| **5. Reassurance** | | |
| ☐ System for providing support determined | | |
| ☐ Marketing representatives know who to call | | |
| ☐ Support is available and timely | | |
| ☐ Challenging questions/situations are being handled effectively | | |
| **6. RSVPs** | | |
| ☐ System for RSVPs determined | | |
| ☐ RSVPs confirmed | | |
| **7. Reports** | | |
| ☐ System for compiling and issuing reports determined | | |
| ☐ Specific check-in points established | | |
| ☐ Submission of results is timely | | |
| ☐ Acknowledgments/thank-yous going out promptly | | |
| ☐ Reports are timely and distributed to: | | |

_____

_____

_____

_____

_____

_____

## Checklist for Reward, Recognition, and Reenlistment Coordinators

| Step | Dates | Notes |
|---|---|---|
| **1. Intangible rewards** | | |
| ☐ Ideas for reminding marketing representatives of value and importance of their efforts are finalized; further creativity encouraged | | |
| ☐ Implementation of ideas is occurring | | |
| ☐ All those working on the effort are rewarded | | |
| **Tangible rewards** | | |
| ☐ Ideas for tangible rewards finalized | | |
| ☐ Group rewards implemented | | |
| ☐ Individual rewards implemented | | |
| ☐ Creative ideas passed along | | |
| **2. Formal Recognition** | | |
| ☐ System for coming up with individualized recognition determined | | |
| ☐ Standard recognition items chosen and ordered | | |
| ☐ Standard recognition items received | | |
| ☐ Individualized recognition items chosen | | |
| ☐ Individualized recognition items obtained | | |
| ☐ Where, when, and how formal recognition will occur is planned | | |
| ☐ Formal recognition plans forwarded to celebration coordinator | | |
| ☐ Follow-up plan for non-attendees determined | | |
| ☐ All formal recognition completed | | |
| **3. Reenlist** | | |
| ☐ Reenlistment discussion occurs | | |
| ☐ Reenlistment decisions and assignments made | | |
| ☐ Reenlistment completed | | |

**SECTION 1—Checklist for Celebration Coordinators**

| Step | Dates | Notes |
|------|-------|-------|
| **1. Determine celebration concept** | | |
| ☐ Type of party/event determined | | |
| ☐ Date and time set | | |
| ☐ Desired location chosen | | |
| ☐ Food and beverage decisions made | | |
| ☐ Ideas for skits, music, or other entertainment chosen | | |
| ☐ Formal recognition to occur at celebration planned and confirmed | | |
| ☐ Ideas for a festive spirit discussed and chosen | | |
| **2. Handle logistics** | | |
| ☐ Invitations designed | | |
| ☐ Invitation list finalized | | |
| ☐ Invitations out | | |
| ☐ Locations confirmed | | |
| ☐ Room(s) checked for size, seating, audiovisual equipment, and other needed capabilities | | |
| ☐ Programs or other written materials determined and in production | | |
| ☐ Food and beverages ordered | | |
| ☐ Decorations and other festive spirit ideas arranged | | |
| ☐ Recognition program finalized | | |
| ☐ Music, other entertainment confirmed | | |
| ☐ Necessary staffing, speakers confirmed | | |
| ☐ RSVPs in | | |
| ☐ Attendance list finalized | | |
| ☐ Materials ready | | |
| ☐ Recognition items ready | | |
| ☐ Final counts to caterers, etc. | | |
| ☐ Name tags ready | | |
| ☐ Final confirmations completed | | |
| ☐ Ready to party! | | |

**SECTION 2—Evaluate the Promotion Effort**

A. Did we achieve our goals?

| Original Goals | Final Results | Percent of Original |
|---|---|---|
| | | |

1. What factors outside our control contributed to these results?

2. What factors within our control contributed to these results?

**SECTION 2—Evaluate the Promotion Effort**

**B. Did we implement our effort effectively?**

Name: _____    Coordination role: _____

1. Were plans followed? If not, what was added or dropped?

2. What went well?

3. Where did you or others you worked with run into problems?

4. What are your recommendations for the future?

## SECTION 2—Evaluate the Promotion Effort

### C. Perspectives of others

| Comments | Source |
|---|---|
| For example: | |
| 1. *Recruitment training needs to be scheduled to give recruiters at least three weeks to do their job.* | 1. *Recruiters* |
| 2. *Additional key messages needed for corporate gatekeepers* | 2. *Solicitors on advance gift meetings* |

## SECTION 2—Evaluate the Promotion Effort

**D. What do we need to refine or research for the future?**

Evaluation may result in clear conclusions that refinements are needed or in questions that require research before effective adjustments can be determined.

**Refinements or research questions**

1. Regarding the scope of the effort

2. Regarding the Marketing Task Force

3. Regarding goals, targeting, message, and communications strategies

4. Regarding roles, people to be involved, the recruitment plan

5. Regarding the master timeline and action plan

*(continued)*

**SECTION 2—Evaluate the Promotion Effort**

6. Regarding the recruitment of marketing representatives

7. Regarding the motivational meetings and training sessions

8. Regarding follow-up and support

9. Regarding rewards, recognition, and reenlistment

10. Regarding celebrating success

11. Regarding evaluation

**SECTION 2—Evaluate the Promotion Effort**

**E. Did we learn and change?**

1. What did people learn from the effort?

2. How did our organization change for the better?

## SECTION 2—Evaluate the Promotion Effort

**F. What are our next steps?**

How will evaluation findings be passed on to inform future efforts?

| Person to receive findings | Person to deliver them | By when |
|---|---|---|
| | | |
| | | |
| | | |
| | | |
| | | |
| | | |
| | | |
| | | |
| | | |
| | | |
| | | |
| | | |
| | | |
| | | |
| | | |
| | | |
| | | |
| | | |

## Collaboration Handbook: Creating, Sustaining, and Enjoying the Journey

*by Michael Winer and Karen Ray*

Shows you how to get a collaboration going, define the results you're after, determine everyone's roles, create an action plan, and evaluate the results. Tells you what to expect and how to handle challenges in a way that strengthens your group. Includes a case study of one collaboration from start to finish, helpful tips on how to avoid pitfalls, and worksheets to keep everyone on track.

*192 pages, softcover, $28.00*

## Collaboration: What Makes It Work

*by Wilder Research Center*

An in-depth review of current collaboration research in the health, social science, education, and public affairs fields. Major findings are summarized, critical conclusions drawn, and nineteen key factors influencing successful collaborations are identified. See if your collaboration's plans include the necessary ingredients.

*53 pages, softcover, $14.00*

## Community Building: What Makes It Work

*by Wilder Research Center*

Shows you what really does (and doesn't) contribute to community building success. Reveals 28 keys to help you build community more effectively and efficiently. Includes detailed descriptions of each factor, case examples of how they play out, and practical questions you can use to assess your work.

*112 pages, softcover, $20.00*

## Coping with Cutbacks

*by Emil Angelica and Vincent Hyman*

The welfare reform act of 1996 is just the tip of the iceberg. The partnership between nonprofits and the federal government is changing. This book helps you understand why and how this is occurring—and what you can do to prepare.

## Marketing Workbook for Nonprofit Organizations Volume I: Develop the Marketing Plan

*by Gary J. Stern*

Don't just wish for results—get them! This book shows you how to create a straightforward, usable marketing plan. It includes the 6 P's of Marketing—and how to use them effectively—a sample marketing plan, and detachable worksheets.

*132 pages, softcover, $25.00*

## Strategic Planning Workbook for Nonprofit Organizations, Revised and Updated

*by Bryan Barry*

Chart a wise course for your nonprofit's future. This time-tested workbook gives you practical step-by-step guidance, real-life examples, one nonprofit's complete strategic plan, and easy-to-use worksheets.

*144 pages, softcover, $25.00*

## The Little Book of Peace

A pocket-size guide to help people think about violence and talk about it with their families and friends.

*24 pages, .65 each (minimum order 10 copies)*

## What Works in Preventing Rural Violence

*by Wilder Research Center*

An in-depth review of 88 effective strategies to respond to rural violence. Also includes a Community Report Card with step-by-step directions on how you can collect, record, and use information about violence in your community.

*94 pages, softcover, $17.00*

## Foundations for Violence-Free Living

A Step-by-Step Guide to Facilitating Men's Domestic Abuse Groups

*by David J. Mathews, MA, LICSW*

A complete guide to facilitating a men's domestic program. Includes 29 activities, detailed guidelines for presenting each activity, and a discussion of psychological issues that may arise out of each activity. Also gives you tips for intake, individual counseling, facilitating groups, working with resistant clients, and recommended policies and releases.

*240 pages, softcover, $45.00*

## On the Level

(Participant's Workbook to Foundations for Violence-Free Living)

Contains 49 worksheets including midterm and final evaluations. Men can record their insights and progress. A permanent binding makes the workbook easy to carry home for outside assignments, and you don't have to make any trips to the copy machine.

*160 pages, softcover, $15.00*

## Journey Beyond Abuse

A Step-by-Step Guide to Facilitating Women's Domestic Abuse Groups

*by Kay-Laurel Fischer and Michael F. McGrane*

Create a program where women increase their understanding of the dynamics of abuse, feel less alone and isolated, feel empowered to make positive choices, and have a greater awareness of channels to safety. Complete tools for facilitating effective groups.

*208 pages, softcover, $45.00*

## Moving Beyond Abuse

(Companion guided journal to Journey Beyond Abuse)

A series of stories and questions that coordinate with the sessions provided in the facilitator's guide. The journal can be used in coordination with a women's group or with the guidance of a counselor in other forms of support for dealing with abuse issues. The open-ended questions provide gentle direction toward gaining insights that help affirm inner strength and heal the wounds of abuse.

*88 pages, softcover, $10.00*

## Four easy ways to order

**Call** toll-free: **1-800-274-6024**
8:00 am to 4:00 pm CST
(in Mpls./St. Paul: 612-659-6024)

**Fax** order form to: **612-642-2061** (24 hours a day)

**Mail** order form to: A. H. Wilder Foundation
Publishing Center
919 Lafond Avenue
St. Paul, MN 55104

**E-mail** your order to: **books@wilder.org**

## Shipping

Standard Charges:

| If order totals: | Add: |
|---|---|
| Up to $30.00 | $4.00 |
| $30.01 - 60.00 | $5.00 |
| $60.01 - 150.00 | $6.00 |
| $150.01 - 500.00 | $8.00 |
| Over $500.00 | 3% of order |

- Orders are shipped UPS or Parcel Post. Please allow two weeks for delivery.
- For orders outside the U.S. or Canada, please add an additional U.S. $5.00
- Special RUSH delivery is available. Please call our toll-free phone number for rates.

## Save money when you order in quantity

We offer substantial discounts on orders of ten or more copies of any single title. Please call for more information.

## Send us your manuscript

Wilder Publishing Center continually seeks manuscripts and proposals for publications in the fields of nonprofit management and community building. Send us your proposal or manuscript. Or, if you'd like more information, call us at 1-800-274-6024 and ask for our Author Guidelines.

## Visit our website at www.wilder.org

---

## Order Form

Prices subject to change

| | QTY. | PRICE EACH | TOTAL AMOUNT |
|---|---|---|---|
| Collaboration Handbook: Creating, Sustaining, and Enjoying the Journey | | $28.00 | |
| Collaboration: What Makes It Work | | 14.00 | |
| Community Building: What Makes It Work | | 20.00 | |
| Coping with Cutbacks | | 25.00 | |
| Foundations for Violence-Free Living | | 45.00 | |
| On the Level (participant's workbook to Foundation's for Violence-Free Living) | | 15.00 | |
| Journey Beyond Abuse (facilitator's guide) | | 45.00 | |
| Moving Beyond Abuse (participant's journal) | | 10.00 | |
| The Little Book of Peace          (minimum order 10 copies) | | 0.65 | |
| Marketing Workbook for Nonprofit Organizations Volume I: Develop the Marketing Plan | | 25.00 | |
| Marketing Workbook for Nonprofit Organizations Volume II: Mobilize People for Marketing Success | | 25.00 | |
| Pocket Guide for Marketing Representatives | | 1.95 | |
| Strategic Planning Workbook for Nonprofit Organizations, Revised and Updated | | 25.00 | |
| What Works in Preventing Rural Violence | | 17.00 | |
| | | **SUBTOTAL** | |
| In MN, please add 7% sales tax or attach exempt certificate | | | |
| | | **SHIPPING** | |
| | | **TOTAL** | |

Amherst H. Wilder Foundation
Publishing Center
919 Lafond Avenue
St. Paul, MN 55104

**Toll-Free 1-800-274-6024**
Fax: (612) 642-2061

**Payment Method:** VISA  MasterCard  AMERICAN EXPRESS Cards

Name _____

Organization _____

Address _____

_____

City _____ State _____ Zip _____

Phone (in case we have questions) (_____) _____

Card # _____

Expiration Date _____

Signature (required) _____

☐ Check/Money Order (payable to A.H. Wilder Foundation)

☐ Bill Me (for orders under $100) Purchase Order # _____